A History of the Baths at Buxton

The Hot Baths, Buxton.

by

Mike Langham

and

Colin Wells

Published by

CHURNET VALLEY BOOKS

43 Bath Street
Leek
Staffordshire
01538 399033

ISBN 1 897949 31 6

Printed in Great Britain by The Ipswich Book Company, Suffolk.

'...Hither the Sick, the Lame, and Barren come,
And hence go healthful, sound and fruitful home.
Buxton's in Beauty famous; but in this
Much more, the Pilgrim never frustrate is,
That comes to bright St Anne...'
Charles Cotton
'The Wonders of the Peake' 1681

'...The custom of attending on watering places, as they
are called, is often attributed to fashion, and has been
exposed in severe terms, as an improper desertion of
business and family affairs. In some instances this may
be the case, and in such it deserves to be reprobated in
the strongest language. In general, however, many and
great allowances are to be made for these excursions.'
Dr Jos Denman MD 1801.

Acknowledgments

We are grateful to the people who have helped in the preparation of this book. The original idea came from Brian George who has done some useful work himself on the Natural Baths. The staff at the Local Studies section of the Buxton library and at the Buxton Museum and Art Gallery are now used to our many and regular enquiries which they always answer in a very helpful way.

We are privileged to have access to the important Devonshire Buxton archive through Tom Askey, the archivist and Peter Day, the Keeper of Collections at Chatsworth.

We thank Martin Bailey of the High Peak Borough who has explained a good deal to us about water management, Richard Tuffrey, the Borough Conservation Officer for his continuing support and Marian McEwan and her staff at the TIC. Nick Dege of the Perrier Group has given us useful information. We are fortunate in having access to research by Ray Bradshaw on the operation of the baths in this present century and we thank him for the valuable contribution this has made to chapter four.

It has now become an important routine for us to ask our friend, and noted local historian, Oliver Gomersal to critically appraise our work and this he has done in his usual careful manner. So we have spent a number of Saturday afternoons getting down to detailed editing, aided by Margery Gomersal who not only sustains us with tea and delicious cake but has also provided first hand descriptions of her own experiences of the baths in the present century.

We are grateful to the staff at Churnet Valley Books in Leek for helping us to place this book before you.

Finally we want to make special mention of the work put into this project by our good friend Ian Clements who has produced a number of quite exceptional original drawings and plans.

Permission to reproduce images has been given as follows:

The Director of Sheffield Leisure Services (Sheffield Archives) for Barker's Plan, (Barker Deeds 666)

The Bodleian Library, Oxford for Prospect of Buxton, (MS. Top. gen. d. 14, fol. 19r) and Buxton Bath July 1712, (MS. Top. gen. e. 61, fol. 14r)

The John Carr plans, by courtesy of the trustees of Sir John Soane's Museum, London

The Bath Archæological Trust have kindly loaned the image of the Roman bath at Bath

Mr Guy De La Bedoyere and BT Batsford Ltd for illustration taken from 'Roman Villas and the Countryside' 1993

EM & GJ Barton

The 1803/6 White plan (map 2042) and F. Langley's 1915 plan of the Natural Baths, are from the Devonshire Collection, reproduced by permission of the Chatsworth Settlement Trustees

The Journals of the Derbyshire Archæological Society

Buxton Museum, the Derbyshire County Council   We thank them all.

All other illustrations are from the authors' collections.

MJL & CW Buxton,
Spring 1997.

PROLOGUE

The water and its origins

Buxton has become famous through the years for its natural thermal water and it is difficult to imagine how the town would have developed without this near-unique natural resource. Only one other British watering place, Bath, can boast a natural thermal water although the water there emerges from the ground at a considerably higher temperature than that at Buxton. The definition of a Thermal Water by the Institute of Geological Sciences, is '...*those waters, which at their point of emergence have the same or a greater temperature than the mean average for the surrounding air...*'

Buxton water emerges from several springs, covering an area of roughly one acre at a constant temperature of 82°F (27.5°C). The origin of the water has been a subject of conjecture throughout history, but modern consensus favours the theory that rainfall to the east of the town sinks down through the limestone layers to a great depth and rises again to the surface under hydrostatic pressure. It is deduced that a fault line exists in the limestone, running north-north-east, continuing over the site of the springs and providing a water route to the surface. Measurements of the tritium content indicate that the water has been underground for many, possibly thousands, of years. The unusually high temperature of the water can be attributed to it rising from a great depth where it is geothermally heated by the earth's interior. With the water rise bubbles of gas, mostly nitrogen and carbon dioxide. Analyses of the water have been conducted over the years with varying levels of accuracy but the main constituent is calcium and this is not surprising, given the terrain. A present day analysis appears in appendix 2.

Chalybeate Water

In addition to the thermal water, the town has at least one chalybeate spring which emerges from a narrow band of shale lying between the limestone and gritstone formations on the north side of the Crescent. Chalybeate or ferruginous water contains iron and was used as a general tonic for anaemic conditions and as an eye bath. It was exploited up until the middle part of the 20th century, but today sites of the springs are not easy to locate and the water is no longer available to us.

Explanatory Notes

(1) Orientation - The Crescent in Buxton faces south east but, for reasons of clarity in describing the positions of buildings in its locality, we have used the assumption that it faces south. This should help in interpreting the direct quotes of some of the early writers who assumed that the Crescent faced south.

(2) Location of principal baths - The principal baths in the Crescent have been described over the years by historians who have used various names. To avoid confusion we have adopted the convention of calling the original baths at the west end of the Crescent, the Natural Baths, and those at the east end of the Crescent, the Hot Baths.

(3) St Anne - As no standard exists for the spelling of the Buxton saint, the earlier form Anne has been adopted throughout in preference to Ann except where the name appears in a direct quotation.

(4) Treatments described - Throughout this book reference is made to particular forms of treatment undertaken by those visiting the baths. In appendix 1 we have attempted to identify the names and describe the many kinds of treatments available at Buxton.

(5) Temperature measurement - Since this is a history we have adopted the convention of quoting temperatures in degrees Fahrenheit with the more modern Celsius measurement in brackets thus: 63.8°F (17.7°C). The equations we have used for conversion are given in appendix 3.

Outside the Hot Baths about 1910

Chapter One

Earliest users of the Water

Archaeological excavations in the 1980s have shown that the earliest settlement known in Buxton dates to the late Mesolithic (Middle Stone Age) period about 5300 BC. These excavations, on Lismore fields, also showed occupation sometime during the Neolithic, or New Stone Age, period (3500-1800 BC)[1]. Other archaeological research has identified Neolithic burial tombs and henge monuments near Buxton and stone circles and barrows associating Buxton with settlements through the Beaker and Bronze Ages to the Iron Age people known as the Celts[2]. The warm springs would no doubt have been known to these peoples.

The Roman name for Buxton was Aquae Arnemetiae, the term 'aquae', meaning mineral springs or waters, was used to describe only one other settlement, that of Bath in Somerset (Aquae Sulis). The Romans tolerated and actually incorporated local cults into their beliefs and Buxton's Roman name means the mineral springs at the sacred grove of the Goddess Arnemetia who was one of the minor Celtic deities. This suggests that there may have been a Celtic settlement close to the warm springs.

Roman Remains

The earliest firm evidence of the existence of a bath using the thermal waters occurs in Roman times and it is likely that Buxton was a Romano British settlement of some significance. The town stands on the intersection of a number of important Roman roads, the evidence for roads connecting Buxton (Aquae Arnemetiae) with forts at Derby (Little Chester); Brough (Anavio); Manchester (Mamucium); Melandra (Ardotalia) and, possibly, Chesterton via Leek has been set out by Wroe[3]. Roman finds on the Silverlands include a Roman milestone discovered in 1856 (but not reported until 1862) which was dug up near a gateway leading to the later London & North Western railway goods station in Higher Buxton. The inscription, according to Tristram translates as: '...*Invested with the power of a Tribune - Consul for the*

Right (proper).   Full front.   Left (proper).

Three views of the Roman milestone found at Buxton

second time - Father of his Country - To Anavio twelve thousand paces', which is twelve Roman miles[4]. During the construction of Holker road, in about 1898, Roman finds included bronze axes and an earthenware vessel, and later finds on Silverlands have included Samian ware pottery, Roman glass and fragments of bronze, iron and lead. It has been concluded from these and other finds, including the presence of hearths and remains of querns, that there was a Romano British settlement on the Silverlands. A comparison of the quality of pottery found on Silverlands with that discovered by Micah Salt at a cave in Deep Dale, about 3 miles from Buxton, has led to the further suggestion that Roman people of some wealth occupied Buxton since the Deep Dale cave appears to have been used by those who had fled from Buxton when under attack[5/6].

There is good recent evidence of a Romano British settlement at Staden, just south of the town, which consisted of a collection of homesteads with enclosures forming courtyards, and a cultivated field system. The evidence suggests mixed farming generating enough wealth for the occupants to enjoy luxuries such as wine and jewellery and the likelihood that this settlement supplied the spa at Buxton[7]. Other recent evidence has emerged from excavations at Poole's Cavern, the show cave in Buxton, where extensive finds suggest Roman occupation from the first to the third centuries AD. Most importantly, the large numbers of brooches and the wide variety of pottery found offer evidence for one of the few sites in Britain of Roman jewellery manufacture and a bronze smithy[8].

Given this evidence for a settlement and the Roman practice of defence through a series of forts connected by well made roads, it has been assumed that Buxton would have had a fort. Three possible sites have been put forward, one by Edward Tristram in 1916 who argued for a fort sited at the top of Bath Road[9]. His argument, based mainly on the elevation and defensive position of the site and the possible junction of Roman roads, is not strong however, and we know of no further fieldwork on his theory. More generally it has been felt that the fort site is most likely to have been on the naturally defensive plateau of Silverlands, and this has been the area of a good deal of excavation, some of which we have already described. More recent evidence, which includes aerial photography, has proved negative and a review by the Trent & Peak Archaeological trust which includes their own excavation work on the site of the former Girls' School has led to the conclusion that no Roman fort existed in the Silverlands area[10]. The third suggested site is the Market Place which has yielded some Roman finds - it offers a large undisturbed area. Senior's map of 1631 shows it as a large rectangular open space, and the possible junction of roads lends some support but, in the absence of firmer evidence, it must remain in the realms of speculation.

The fort has so far proved elusive, but there is evidence for a substantial and wealthy settlement which supports the case for a Roman spa, a centre for rest and recuperation probably for both a military and civilian population. Given this proposition we should look carefully at the evidence for a Roman bathing complex.

Roman Baths

Remains of a Roman bath were reported by Dr Charles Leigh writing in 1700 after one of his visits to Buxton when he described '...*a Roman Wall cemented with red Roman Plaister, close by St Ann's Well, where we may see the Ruines of the ancient Bath, its Dimensions and Length. This Plaister is red and hard as Brick, a Mixture not prepared in these Days...*'[11]. The difficulty we have with this description is that Leigh does not make clear whether the '*Roman Plaistered Wall*' is the same as the 'Ruines of the ancient Bath'. It seems likely, however, that the wall is the remains of a Roman structure surrounding St Anne's Well, as the physician Thomas Short, writing in 1734, says that: '...*St Anne's well formerly rose up into a stone basin shut up within an ancient Roman brick wall, a yard square within and a yard high on three sides till Sir Thomas Delves built the present Arch over it...*', and his further description confirms the position of St Annes Well '...*twenty four yards north of the outer bath...*'[12]. John Speed's map of 1610 carries an engraving of St Anne's Well which could fit Short's description and position. Recent analysis by Leach[13] suggests that the original St Annes Well was located under the third pier of the western end of the present Crescent.

Thomas Short also describes the remains of a further bath, '...*About thirty six years ago, when Mr White, then of Buxton Hall, was driving up a Level to the Bath, fifty Yards East of St Anne's Well, and fourteen Yards North of Bingham Spring, the Workmen found buried deep under the Grass and Corn-mould, Sheets of Lead spread upon Great Beams of Timber, about four Yards Square, with broken Ledges round about, which had been a Leaden Cystern, and not unlikely, that of the Romans, or some other antient Bath which had been supplied with Water from the Bingham Well...*'[12]. He is referring, here, to the discovery made by Cornelius White, proprietor of the Hall who made a number of improvements to the Hall and Baths in 1695/6. However, Sir John Floyer MD writing in 1697 offers a more contemporaneous account of White's improvements which differs from Short in a number of important ways, '...*New Improvements at Buxton Baths AD 1695 and 1696 by Cornelius White...By taking off some of the cold Springs from the hot, the antient Bath repaired and paved, and a new one made for the better conveniency of the poor and impotent; And a sough about 200 yards in length to drain both, for the cleaning thereof every day...About the middle of the Sough a Cistern of lead was found two yards square, and one foot deep, being four yards within the earth, supported by several oaken planks: Something higher in the same Sough, was found a place seven Yards wide, and twenty Yards long, being smooth and even on both sides and at the bottom, two Yards deep in the Earth and made of Stone...*'[14]. Floyer's account is important on three counts. Firstly he mentioned improvements to the ancient bath which we take to be the one adjacent to the Hall. Secondly he described the lead bath or cistern as six feet square by one foot deep buried 12 feet under the ground. This is half the size of that described by Short. Thirdly he described a much larger structure which might be a bath but could be foundations for something else since he described it as a 'place' and gave insufficient measurements for a bath, but indicated that it was buried six feet under the ground.

Another discovery was made in 1781 during the building of the Crescent when a new tepid spring was identified close to the remains of a rectangular bath 15' x 30'. The floor of the bath was of red plaster 6' thick with a boat shaped cavity at one end; the water entered at the west end through a wide lead pipe and exited at the east end through a floodgate. The bath wall was 3' high and constructed of limestone covered with a strong cement, and strong oak beams were laid on the top of the walls firmly connected together at the corners. The location of this bath was 6 yards from the Bath Room which, in 1781, was the room housing the main inner bath adjacent to the Hall. The medical doctor, Jos Denman, writing in 1793, gave a similar description but was sceptical of the extent of Roman finds inferring that contemporary writers had tended to embroider the facts a little. Paradoxically, he gave the recollections of two men who worked on the building of the Crescent which add more to the original description. They confirm the size and shape of the bath but add that 10 feet from the bath on the north side was what they thought to be a drinking well built of gritstone which had a flight of steps more than 7 feet deep[15]. Pearson, writing in 1784, used the findings of a Mr Watson, who in 1780 described two baths. In the larger one with the plaster floor, he said there were some bottles, supposedly Roman; the second bath was smaller and had a wall of stone[16].

A further and most important find was made in August 1975, during reconstruction work on the floor of the 20th century swimming pool, situated over hot and cold springs in the Natural baths. A brick structure was unearthed, together with 232 Roman coins, 3 bronze bracelets and a wire clasp. Subsequent research suggests that these were offerings to the Celtic god Arnemetia and the dates of the coins which range largely from 100 AD to 400 AD indicate these offerings were made throughout the period of Roman occupation. Close by the Roman deposit, jewellery spanning the 16th to 18th centuries was found, together with a large number of 17th century pins which were also used as offerings[2].

Roman Spa Complex

The difficulty in analysing this evidence is that the early writers differ in their descriptions of size and location of remains. Great care is needed in determining the orientation of directions given and more detailed work is needed to site the bath remains with any degree of precision. Nevertheless, it is possible to suggest that there

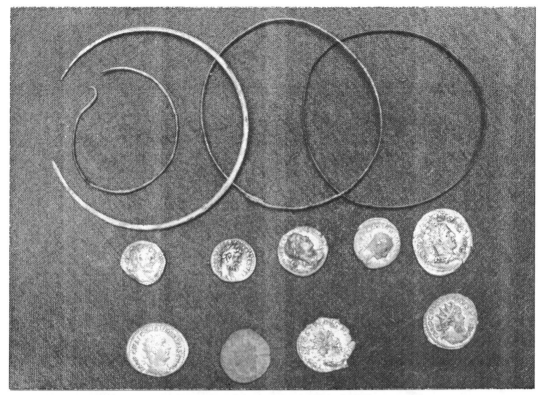

Examples of the votive coin find of 1975

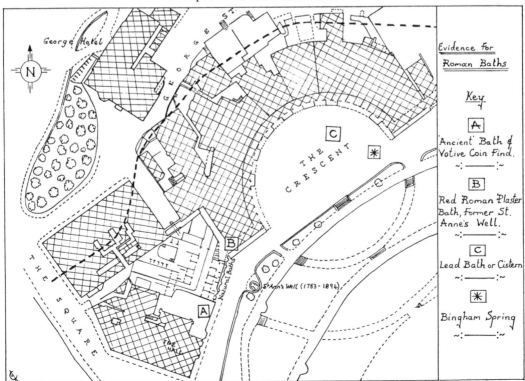

Evidence for Roman baths

were broadly three areas over the spring sources forming the sites of Roman baths. These would correspond today to: (A) the Natural Baths area where the votive coin find and the references in early writings to an 'ancient bath' suggest Roman use; (B) the western wing of the Crescent where we have the remains found in 1781 and the St.Anne's Well observations of 1700 and more recently; (C) east of the centre of the Crescent where the lead bath remains were unearthed in 1697.

Given this evidence what, typically, might a Roman bath complex at Aquae Arnemetiae have looked like? The most usual provision in public baths was a route involving three types of bath, tepid [Tepidarium], hot [Calidarium] and cold [Frigidarium]. These would be built into a complex which included changing rooms with niches for clothes, a latrine and a furnace for heating the water. The warm, wet atmosphere created by the baths gave rise to high levels of building maintenance and, for this reason, the roofs of bath houses were often barrel-vaulted. A good example of such baths at Beauport Park in Sussex, associated with a large settlement concerned with iron ore extraction, has been described in detail by Bedoyere in a recent study[17].

Buxton (Aquae Arnemetiae), as we have already noted, shares the name 'aquae', meaning waters or mineral springs, with Bath in Somerset (Aquae Sulis) and it is interesting to speculate whether Buxton might have had a modest version of the temple and baths complex at Bath. A reconstruction of Roman Bath shows the sacred spring covered with a barrel-vaulted roof, forming a focal point of a religious complex with the classical temple of Sulis-Minerva

A reconstructed isometric view of a
Roman bath house at Beauport Park, Sussex.
A: Changing room.
B: Warm rooms.
C: Hot rooms.
D: Cold bath.
E: Disused furnace.
F: Furnace   *Taken from Bedoyere, 1993*

alongside, the two buildings being set inside a walled precinct. Adjacent to the spring, but outside the precinct, was a complex of baths some with barrel-vaulted roofs. Distribution of the water from the spring source to the baths involved the use of lead pipes and reservoirs built of stone on timber piles and lead lined. The Great Bath was also lead lined. Buxton has the remains of such bath materials and the votive coin find offers evidence of worship to at least one deity, the Goddess Arnemetia. There is other, though limited, evidence of a possible shrine on Staincliffe (the Slopes) given by Major Rooke's archaeological findings in 1787/8, though his research is considered weak. The

Reconstruction of the Roman baths at Bath

possibilities are there but much archaeological work would be required around the spring sources and the Slopes to begin to verify the scenario we have suggested. However, taking all the available evidence set out in this chapter it is entirely reasonable to propose that extensive commercial exploitation of the natural warm and cold springs took place in Roman Buxton.

Anglo Saxon and Danish

The Romans withdrew their government of Britain in about 410 AD, leaving the native Romano Britons to face invasion by the Angles, Saxons and Jutes of Northern Germany and Denmark, who settled initially in the more fertile south and east. Movement into the Peak District took place via the Rivers Trent, Derwent and Dove in the late sixth century and the Rivers Mersey, Etherow and Goyt in the seventh century. The many small tribes which made up the invasions gradually formed into seven separate kingdoms. One of these, Mercia (meaning 'borderland'), extended over the greater part of the Midlands and included North Derbyshire. A surviving document called the Tribal Hidage, drawn up in the mid to late 7th century, probably to assess the taxable value of Mercia, tells us that the settlers in North Derbyshire were known as Pecsaetan or 'Peak-dwellers'. The northern border of Mercia was with the Northumbrians, led by King Eadwine (Edwin) who brought Christianity to Northumbria through the priest Paulinus, and built a church at York. The first recorded Christian missionary in Mercia was Paulinus, who preached and baptised at Littleborough (Notts) in 627. The existence of place names in the Peak District such as Eccles Cross and Eccles Pike, suggest sites of early British Christianity, the term eccles denoting this, but the invading Anglo Saxons were pagan. Thus when Christianity reached the Peak Dwellers in the mid 7th century it was, in some part, a reintroduction. The Roman road from the River Trent to Buxton guided the early Anglian settlers on their way north, the concentration of barrow burials along this road, including the very important finds at Benty Grange, confirm this. During the 8th century it is likely that the baths were in a state of disrepair. There is a piece of Anglo Saxon poetry called 'The Ruin', which is thought to be describing the hot springs at Bath but which gives us a feel for how Buxton baths might have looked:

'...Well wrought this wall: Fate broke it. Bright were the buildings, Halls where springs ran...stood stone houses: wide streams welled hot from source and a wall all caught in its bright bosom...' [18].

Mercia was annexed by the invading Vikings in 874, who founded the new borough of Derby, and Buxton was presumably accessible via the Roman road. The reconquest of the area in about 920, by Edward the Elder, resulted in the building of a fort in Bakewell and by 966, when Edgar had united the two kingdoms of Britain north and south of the River Thames to become the 'king of the whole of Britain', the area incorporating Bakewell, Ashford and Hope was a single region of some wealth. During this period of nearly 700 years we can only speculate that the warm springs of Buxton would have been been used for bathing, if not for curative purposes. Whilst there is no firm archaeological or written evidence for this, the later use of the springs suggests a continuing line of use throughout this period.

Mediaeval Springs and Shrine

There is no mention of Buxton in the Domesday survey of 1086 though Wormhill (Wruenele) and Tideswell (Tideswelle) are both included. However, since the survey was an administrative exercise designed to inform King William of the wealth of his kingdom, it set out to identify estates which could produce a taxable income. The last question asked by his commissioners is telling, '*...Can more be got?*' Buxton at the beginning of the 12th century was primarily a cattle pasturing place and may have been so at the time of the Domesday survey. Archaeological and place name evidence for Staden, just outside Buxton, suggests a mediaeval settlement dating from the early 12th century including a longhouse[7]. At this time William Peveril gave land to found Lenton Abbey in Nottinghamshire and the foundation charter dated between 1100-08 gives the origin of Buxton as Buc(k)stanes, though the variation Buchestanes was also known from 1108. The name may derive from bucc and stan meaning buck stones (as in deer) or, more likely, Bug-stan meaning rocking stones[19]. There are a number of variations on the name, for example the term Kyngesbucstones was known by 1366 and suggests that Buxton was associated with the Forest of the Peak. The earliest written evidence we have for a well at Buxton occurs about 1460, when William Worcester, also known as Botoner, wrote an 'itinerarium' of places he had probably visited during his lifetime. He describes Buxton as follows:

> '...*Memorandum that Halywell, the source of the waters of Wye, in the county of Derby, about 100 miles from London, makes many miracles making the infirm healthy, and in winter it is warm, even as honeyed milk....*'[20].

He incorrectly attributes the source of the River Wye to the mineral springs but his description indicates that the well was in use at this time for medicinal purposes and the 'cures' were associated with the warmth of the water but also with religious belief. Further confirmation is given in the 'inquisition post mortem' of John Talbot, second Earl of Shrewsbury, who was killed in the battle of Northampton in 1460. He owned the Manor of Chelmorton, twenty acres of land at Fairfield and '*one rood of land at Bukston juxta Halywell*'.

Access to Buxton would not have been easy at that time, though we know from a legal case of 1490 that there was a road from Ashbourne to Buxton called 'Alsope Way'.[20] It seems likely that a holy well of such repute as Buxton would have had a chapel and, from a will of 1493-4, we learn of Buxtonford Chapel, the earliest mention of a chapel but also suggesting that the River Wye had a ford rather than a bridge.

It is not until 1521, however, that we see the name St Anne being used. The name Anne was uncommon in England until King Richard II married Anne of Bohemia in 1382. Anne, the apocryphal mother of the Virgin Mary, was a cult figure associated with miracles of healing in mediaeval England and the observance of her feast was made obligatory throughout England, by Pope Urban VI, in response to a petition, in that same year. King Richard II may have been in Tideswell between September 1399 and February 1400, prior to his death in Yorkshire, and this has led to the suggestion that the Buxton Well may have been named after his queen. An alternative, but less plausible account, concerns the discovery of a statue of a Goddess by the Cotterell family who came into possession of the land on which the chapel and well stood in 1489. It is suggested that the statue was of the Roman Goddess Arnemetia and the first four letters inscribed on it were misread as Anne. Dr John Jones, writing in 1572 was sceptical. However, he wrote; '...*and as for Cotterell's tale, or the vayne invencions about S. Anne found in the well, or of the water set from flood Jordan, I reckon them not worthy the recital. Therefore I will not detayne you with such tryfles...*'[21]. This may have been a tale, then, put out by the Cotterells to drum up business, though we know there was an image of St Anne removed from the well chapel in 1538.

The detailed household accounts kept by the steward of Sir Henry Willoughby (an ancestor of Lord Middleton) between 1521-26 suggest visits by the gentry at Buxton:

> *'...Item Tuesday the 27 of June for your reward to two women that washed lead ore as ye went to Saint Anne's 2d.*
> *Item for my Master's costs at Saint Anne's of Bucstone, the 7th day of September, 7s. 6d.*
> *Item for my Master's offering to Saint Anne's sent by Clyfton, 4d.'*[20].

From this time there is much evidence for the continuing use of the waters. In 1569 a play written by John Heywood, a Londoner, included St Anne of Buxton as one of a number of sacred shrines and the famous, and perhaps earliest, English antiquary John Leland who travelled between 1533 and 1539, included '*S.Anne of Bukstanes Welle*' in his account. In 1535 King Henry VIII instituted a national enquiry to determine the value of the church's wealth, prior to the dissolution of the monasteries, but no information could be obtained about the value of offerings at the shrine. However, in about the same year the jewels, goods and chattels at the Well were the subject of a legal dispute between the executors of the Vicar of Bakewell and the Chaplain of Buxton, Thomas Turner, in which their value was given as forty marks [£26] and it may be because of this that the value of the offerings was kept from the commissioners.

The Well and chapel did not escape the attention of Thomas Cromwell, King Henry's chief minister during the dissolution, and in 1538 he gave orders for Sir William Bassett of Langley to dismantle the chapel and Well. This was speedily done, Bassett writing to Lord Cromwell saying, '*...My Lord I have allso lockkyd upp and sealyd the bathys and welles att Buxtone thatt none schall enter...*'[22], and he also took the statue of Saint Anne, which was forwarded to Cromwell's place near Austin Friars in London. Sir William Bassett's letter tells us that the chapel contained the offerings of those seeking a cure and that he had ordered the keeper that no more offerings should be made. His letter also suggests that the 'bathys and welles' were enclosed otherwise they could not have been sealed up in such a way that no-one could enter. It is likely, however, that they were not closed for long.

In 1541 a judgment was enacted in Chancery requiring Robert and Roger Cotterell to allow a priest to sing and say mass and other divine service in the chapel of Saint Anne. The Cotterells, as we have noted, came into possession of the land on which the chapel and Well stood in 1489 but in the mid 16th century the family were engaged in a number of disputes over the use of the chapel and Well and over who should be entitled to the offerings made there. In 1553-55 the Cotterells were charged with preventing the people of Buxton from using the chapel for divine service, as required in the decree of 1541, also locking up the chapel and taking away the key. Furthermore they had allowed youthful persons to wash and bathe themselves in St Anne's Well, to get drunk within the chapel and to pipe, dance, hop and sing, all to the great disturbance of the inhabitants of Buxton, but most heinously, to do this on a Sunday. The case was heard at Derby and must have been considered serious by the Justice of Assize, for Roger Cotterell was bound over in the sum of £100, a very large amount, and had to pay most of the costs of both sides in the dispute. The Cotterells fought a further case in 1569, from which we learn that they had enjoyed the profits from the Chapel of St Anne with the Wells adjoining for 60 years, though for much of that time it seems that they had been in dispute with the clergy of Bakewell. However, in this same year they sold the Chapel, well and spring grounds, to the sixth Earl of Shrewsbury[23].

Royal Patronage
In the fourth quarter of the 16th century the fame of Buxton and its waters was greatly enhanced by two sets of circumstances. Firstly, in 1572, Dr John Jones published the first known medical treatise on Buxton waters. Secondly and most importantly, Buxton

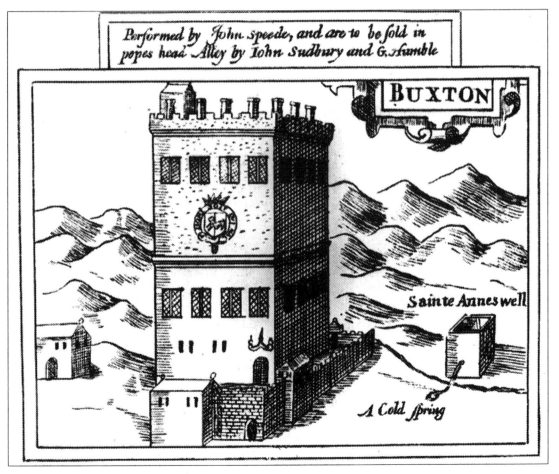

The Buxton Hall, built 1572/3 by the 6th Earl of Shrewsbury [from John Speed's map 1610]

was visited on several occasions between 1573 and 1584 by Mary Queen of Scots.

Dr John Jones' book was entitled, *'The Benefit of the auncient Bathes of Buckstones, which cureth most greevous sicknesses, never before published'*. He described the situation of Buxton and its natural warm and cold springs, indicating rules for bathing including times, length of stay in the bath and diet. He associated the medicinal virtues of the water with religious belief and set out a lengthy prayer to be said at the bath side as part of the bathing regime. Jones referred to three chief baths and said that the first of these chief baths was the warmer spring. He described the Baths as being '...*bravely beautified with Seats round about, and defended from the ambient air, and chimneys for fire to air your Garments in the Bath side, and other Necessaries most decent...*'[21]

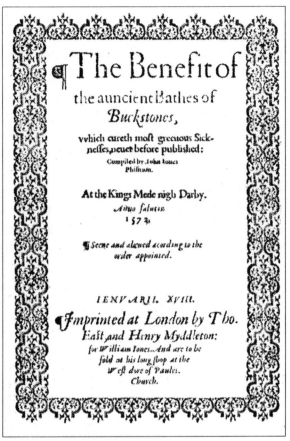

though it is not clear if he is describing here all three baths or just the first chief bath. He also described the new Hall being built by the Earl of Shrewsbury and said that this was adjoining the chief spring between the river and the bath. It is reasonable to conclude that at this time there was a main bath in use, together with two others, one of which was St Anne's Well, the other either a bath or a well.

Dr Jones made a number of recommendations. He argued for a permanent physician to be available and he put forward ideas for assisting the poor, the first mention of a bath charity. His claims for cures obtained through the use of the water were extensive and included, '...*Women that by reason of overmuch moisture, or contrary distemperature bee unapt to conceive.....weake men that be unfrutefull...profitable for such as have the consumption of the lungs.....very good for the inflammation of the liver.....it stayeth wasting of man's seede, the Hemoroydes, and Pyles, it soone amendeth.....for them that be short winded it much availeth.....the greene sickness it perfectly cureth...*'[21]. The book also described the games and pastimes available which included bowling, shooting, wind or yarne ball (a form of handball) and a game called 'Troule in Madam', which consisted of rolling leather or similar balls into slots, rather like rollerball. Dr Jones dedicated his book to the sixth Earl of Shrewsbury and his Countess Elizabeth, (Bess of Hardwick) who were probably his patrons, and it is possible to see this book as an advertisement for a Buxton then being developed by the Earl to attract visitors.

In 1569 the sixth Earl of Shrewsbury, George Talbot, was given custody of Mary, Queen of Scots, an onerous task which was to occupy him for 15 of the almost 19 years she spent in captivity. During that period the Scottish Queen spent time at Sheffield, with visits to Chatsworth, Tutbury Castle, Wingfield and Buxton. She came to Buxton seeking cures for her illnesses which have been variously described as, 'a severe grief of the splene', digestive upsets, headaches, rheumatism and recurring pain in the side. The Earl was a major landowner in northern England and had enhanced his property holdings when he married Bess of Hardwick in 1568. He visited Buxton in 1569 seeking treatment for gout in his hands and legs and, from his own report, benefited greatly from taking the waters. Mary, Queen of Scots, first requested to go to 'Bookston's Well' in 1571 and she renewed her request in 1572 but Queen Elizabeth would not allow a visit, her reason being that the Hall, then being built by the Earl of Shrewsbury, was not ready. Queen Elizabeth was very wary of Mary, Queen of Scots, who was the natural leader of a large Catholic minority and posed a very real challenge to the English throne.

Given the political intrigue and plotting of the time, Buxton, a remote village in the hills, represented a possible safe haven for the Scottish queen and a consequent security risk for Queen Elizabeth. The correspondence between the sixth Earl of Shrewsbury and the royal court, principally Lord Burghley, the Lord Treasurer, reflects the great suspicion with which Queen Elizabeth viewed Mary's visits to Buxton. On 10th August 1573 Lord Burghley wrote to Shrewsbury saying that the Queen was content that he should move Mary, Queen of Scots to Buxton if he could do so without peril and if strangers could be kept away whilst she was there. The Scottish queen came to Buxton in August and September of 1573 and, from written records we know that she returned in 1576, 1580, 1582 and 1584, usually for several weeks in the summer. Like bees around a honey pot she was followed to Buxton by members of the royal court, including very influential figures. Lord Burghley, the Lord Treasurer visited several times and met with the Earl of Shrewsbury who, whilst fulfilling his duties as Queen Mary's gaoler, took the waters for his gout. Other important visitors included Sir Thomas Smith, Secretary of State; Lady Mildmay, wife of Sir Walter, Chancellor of the Exchequer; Lord Gilbert and Lady Mary Talbot; and Sir Thomas Cecil. The most influential visitor by far, however, was Robert Dudley, Earl of Leicester and favourite of Queen Elizabeth[24].

The visits of Mary, Queen of Scots were greatly enjoyed by her and did much to ease her health and low spirits. In 1580 she begged to be allowed to visit Buxton, saying that she had found no remedy better for the complaint in her side. During one of her visits she reputedly visited Poole's Cavern, a noted show cave. Many of the nobility came for a water cure; the Earl of Sussex, for example, drank three pints a day increasing daily by one extra pint until he reached eight pints, then reducing by a pint a day back to three pints. The Earl of Leicester was advised, in July of 1576, that wherever he travelled he must, '...*drink Buxton Water twenty days together...*'[25].

The idea of spending time at baths and wells for healing and relaxation purposes was becoming popular amongst the nobility and gentry at this time. It has been suggested that this new habit was becoming an accepted part of the social routine of the elite with humbler people drawn in their wake and in this way the secular holiday was beginning to emerge[26]. Undoubtedly Bess of Hardwick used her considerable business acumen to promote Buxton as a fashionable watering place and it is clear, from correspondence, that Shrewsbury's Hall was very busy during this time and Buxton was enjoying extensive royal patronage. She had a sharp wit, however, for when the Earl of Leicester left Buxton limping (due to a 'boyle' on his leg), she inquired if Buxton sent sound men home halting![27]

However, not all who visited came just to take the waters. Some, it would seem, came for less innocent reasons. Queen Elizabeth was concerned that Mary had too much access to the outside world. She was fearful that Mary would endear herself to the common people so the Earl of Shrewsbury was constantly harried to ensure that the Scottish Queen was suitably guarded. In 1576 he was obliged to refute the charge that Mary had too much freedom in being allowed to talk to a cripple at the bath and, writing to Lord Burghley in 1580, he gave examples of his strict surveillance at Buxton. In a later letter he said that he was guarding her circumspectly, as the Queen desired and added '...*the desire I have to serve my sovereign makes peril and pain a pleasure to me...*'[28]. There is little doubt, however, that intrigue and plotting was taking place in this remote place in the hills. In 1574 two conspirators, Alexander Hamilton and Henry Cockyn, confessed that they were in Buxton at Whitsuntide and Dr Edward Astlowe, who accompanied the Earl of Sussex to Buxton, was a sympathiser of Mary, later tortured for conspiracy. Buxton may be connected with Mary's ultimate conviction of complicity in the Babington plot, which led to her execution at Fotheringhay Castle in 1587. Sir Anthony Babington was a Derbyshire Squire who lived at Dethick. He was a Roman Catholic, a young man fired with zealous enthusiasm for Mary's cause, and the leader of a group who planned to dethrone Elizabeth in favour of Mary. The early seeds of this plot could have been sown in Buxton for there is evidence, through the confession of a man named Anthony Tyrell, of a meeting of gentlemen and priests at St.Anne of Buckstones at which a rebellion had been planned. Babington and his conspirators were subsequently tried and put to death[28/29].

Much of the evidence we have for Mary, Queen of Scots' association with Buxton

Poole's Cavern, Buxton from Leigh 1700

is in written correspondence, but there is one piece which is quite unique in that it consists of messages by her and others scratched on a window in the Hall. The window itself has, unfortunately, been lost but a copy was kept and '...*Things written in the glasse windowes at Buxstons...*' is now part of the Portland papers at Longleat[30]. The practice of scratching on glass could have been simply a pastime or, conceivably, a way of leaving coded messages for others. The window, which was divided into four columns, contains verse and prose in Latin, French and Greek by Mary, Jaques Nau, her secretary, the Earl of Leicester and others written between 1573 and 1582. The physician to Queen Elizabeth and the Earl of Leicester, Dr Bayley, wrote, '*Hoc tantum scio quod nihil scio*', loosely translated, 'This much I do know, that I know nothing'. We might speculate on whether this is false modesty on the part of the doctor or some more cryptic message[31]. The most often quoted of Queen Mary's sayings does not appear on this window and was scratched on her last visit in 1584. It is quite prophetic:

> *Buxtona quæ calidæ celebrabere nomine lympæ*
> *Forte mihi posthac non adeunda, vale.*
>
> *Buxton whose fame thy milk warm waters tell*
> *Whom I perhaps shall see no more, farewell[32].*

The popularity of Buxton in Tudor times certainly established the reputation of the spa and the fame of the waters caused large numbers of sick poor to visit. In 1595 the people of the village of Fairfield petitioned Queen Elizabeth for permission to maintain a perpetual chapel and priest, citing as part of their case that they were impoverished partly due to contributing to the upkeep of poor sick people who travelled to the baths at Buxton. Two years later, in the 39th year of Queen Elizabeth, an act was passed stipulating that no one resorting to the baths at either Bath (Somerset) or Buxton should be allowed to beg and that poor people should obtain relief from their own parish and travel only with the approval of two Justices of the Peace who were to determine the duration of their visit.

As the reputation of the waters spread, the accommodation at Buxton expanded and a survey of Derbyshire's taverns and inns in 1577 shows that Buxton had the only two inns recorded in the High Peak, together with eight ale houses. One of the inns was the Earl of Shrewsbury's new Hall, which was frequented by the nobility.

Sir Thomas Throckmorton experienced very wet weather in the summer of 1594 and decided Bath in Somerset would be better for him. Roger Manners, 5th Earl of Rutland visiting in 1595 unfortunately saw nothing of commendation apart from the water. The Earl of Shrewsbury, however, took the precaution of giving directions for food to be ready on his arrival in September 1609. Those of lesser means would, no doubt, have found accommodation in the ale houses or inns which, by 1592, included the Eagle and Child, though, as we shall see in the next chapter, the accommodation did not keep pace with the growing popularity of the water treatment.

References
1. Garton, D. Buxton Current Archaeology, No. 103 1987
2. Hart C.R. North Derbyshire Archaeological Survey, Sheffield City Museums, 1984
3. Wroe, P. Roman Roads in the Peak District Derbyshire Archaeological Journal [DAJ} Vol CII 1982
4. Tristram Edward, Roman Buxton Derbyshire Archaeological Journal (DAJ)Vol XXXVIII, 1916
5. Turner W. FSA The Reliquary May 1903
6. Salt WH. Reliquary and Archaeologist, April 1900
7. Makepeace G. The Roman-British Settlement at Staden near Buxton: The 1987-88 and 1989-90 Excavations and Final Report. DAJ. Vol. 115 1995
8. Bramwell D. et al Excavations at Poole's Cavern, DAJ. 1983; also Branigan K. & Bayley J. DAJ. Vol. CIX 1989
9. Tristram Edward, op. cit. pp. 86/7
10. Walker J. Buxton: The Natural Baths, Trent & Peak Archaeological Trust, 1994
11. Leigh, Charles. The Natural History of Lancashire, Cheshire and the Peak in Derbyshire, Oxford 1700
12. Short Thomas, MD. The Natural, Experimental and Medical History of the Mineral Waters of Derbyshire, Lincolnshire and Yorkshire, London 1734.
13. Leach J. Buxton Well Chapel Occasional Paper no. 2, Buxton Archaeological & Natural History Society, Bulletin no. 2 Autumn 1986
14. Floyer Sir John, An Enquiry into the Right Uses and Abuses of the Hot and Cold Temperate Baths in England 1697
15. Denman Jos. MD. Observations on Buxton Water, editions of 1793 and 1801
16. Pearson, George, Observations and Experiments for Investigating the Chymical History of the Tepid Springs of Buxton, London 1784.
17. Bedoyere, Guy de la, Roman Villas and the Countryside, BT Batsford Ltd/English Heritage, London, 1993.
18. Kennedy C. W. The Earliest English Poetry, Oxford University Press, 1943
19. Cameron K. The Place Names of Derbyshire Part I, English Place Name Society, 1993
20. Axon Ernest. Historical Notes on Buxton, its inhabitants and visitors, Paper 3, 1936
21. Jones John. The Benefit of the auncient Bathes of Buckstones, which cureth most greevous sicknesses, never before published. 1572
22 Axon Ernest., op. cit. paper 4, November 1936
23. Axon Ernest., op. cit. paper 5, November 1937
24. Batho G.R. A Calender of the Shrewsbury and Talbot Papers, Vol II, HMSO 1971
25. Ibid. Vol. F Folio 157
26. Hembry, Phyllis, The English Spa 1560-1815, The Athlone Press London, 1990
27. Axon Ernest op. cit. paper 2 1934
28. Ibid. Vol. G Folio 37
29. Fraser Antonia. Mary Queen of Scots, Weidenfeld & Nicolson, 1969
30. Portland papers, Vol. I Folio 105, Longleat House, Warminster
31. Langham, Mike. Things Written in the Glasse Windowes at Buxtons, Derbyshire Miscellany, Spring 1998, Vol 15, Part 1
32. Camden, William, Survey of the County of Derbyshire, 1610

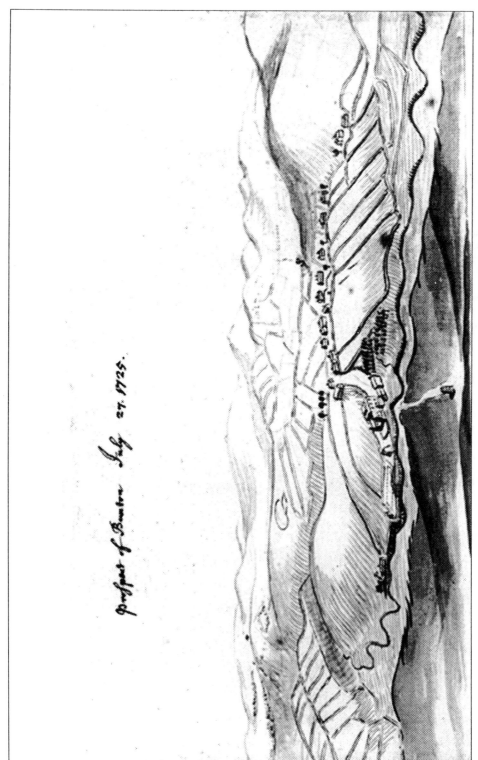

'Prospect of Buxton - July 1725' drawn by William Stukeley. This is a view from Corbar Hill showing Cornelius White's bowling green of 1695/6 at the rear of the Hall, just left of the centre of the picture.

Chapter Two

The Growth of the Spa

From the beginning of the 17th century we see an increasing number of writers describing the waters at Buxton and extolling their virtues. The first English edition of 'Britannia' by the antiquary and historian, William Camden, was published in 1610 and mentioned the value of the hot springs. Between 1613 and 1622 the poet Michael Drayton published an extremely long poem on the history and topography of great Britain called Poly-Olbion and, though much of his information came from Camden's 'Britannia', he offers a fine description of Buxton Wells:

> *'Yet for her caves and holes, Peake onely not excells,*
> *But that I can again produce those wondrous wells*
> *Of Buckston, as I have, that most delicious fount,*
> *Which when the second bath of England doe account*
> *Which in the primer raignes, when first this well began,*
> *To have her vertues knowne unto the blest Saint Anne,*
> *Was consecrated then, which the same temper hath,*
> *As the most daintie spring, which at the famous bath,*
> *Is by the crosse enstild, whose fame I much preferre*
> *In that I doe compare my daintiest spring to her*
> *Nice sickness to cure, as also to prevent,*
> *And supple thier cleare skinnes, which ladies oft frequent;*
> *Most full, most faire, most sweet and most delicious sourse.'[1]*

The votive coin find of 1975, described in the last chapter, included a token, a coin, jewellery and pins spanning the 17th century, which suggests a continuing line of use of the chief bath described by Dr Jones in 1572. The earliest known picture of the Hall and baths occurs on John Speed's map of Derbyshire 1610. The Hall is shown, together with a walled perimeter which, we believe, enclosed the chief bath. St Anne's Well is shown and a further building which may be the well chapel. Speed described nine springs, eight warm and one very cold, which ran from under a fair square building of freestone. About 60 paces away, enclosed with four flat stones, was a well called St Anne's, near to which another very cold spring bubbled up. Justine Paget, a barrister, writing in 1630, confirms the position of the chief bath when he describes the Hall as a pretty little brick house inside which the bath, fed by six hot springs and one cold, was situated in a low room. Since the Hall was not built of brick he is most likely describing the bath building. The following poetic account of a visit to Buxton by the clergyman Richard James in 1636 appears to describe how the hot and cold springs were managed at that time:

> *'Though when I sawe Saint Anne of Buckstones well*
> *Hot with a chimney; for springs colde and warme*
> *Rising together doe the bathing harme...'[2].*

Charles Cotton 1630-87

The seven wonders of the Peak described by Thomas Hobbes, tutor to the Cavendish family, in a book published about 1636[3] and Charles Cotton's 'Wonders of the Peak'[4], did much to publicise the Peak District and the Buxton waters. Cotton's book in particular was very popular and had reached its fourth edition by 1699. It has been long thought, mainly due to the writings of Charles Cotton, that the Hall had been burnt down in 1670 and was left '...*near a ruin...*', being subsequently rebuilt and enlarged by William, third Earl of Devonshire. However, a recent study by the Royal Commission on Ancient Buildings has discovered that the majority of the original 1573 walls of the Hall still remain within today's Old Hall Hotel. This would suggest that the Earl's rebuild was probably not as extensive as previously thought and was probably confined to work on the roof, the windows and other minor alterations[5].

In 1695/6 Cornelius White, landlord of the Hall and Buxton's first lawyer, made further alterations to the Hall and bath. He repaired the inner bath (referred to as the 'Chief' or 'Great' Bath) and drove a level of over 100 yards long from the bath to the River Wye. This enabled the bath to be drained and washed out with fresh water which made for more hygienic bathing. He also built an outer bath on land to the north of the inner bath where an old kitchen stood, which was designed for the use of the 'poor and impotent'. It was called 'White's Bath' and though walled round, was apparently open to the elements. The outer bath dimensions were seventeen feet long by ten foot two inches wide and had a water depth of five feet four inches; it was fed by the overflow from the inner bath and, like the former, was fitted with a sluice in order to empty the bath when necessary. Short[10] says that White fixed a pump in this bath to pump off the cold springs whilst ladies were in the bath but, afterwards, made a sough to carry off the springs entirely so that they did not chill the warm water. In addition to these bath alterations, White built more apartments, new stables adjoining the Hall, gardens and a bowling green.

Despite these improvements it seems that much was lacking in terms of creature comforts both in the Hall and the bath. The intrepid Celia Fiennes who toured Britain on horseback in 1697 says of the Hall;

> '...*The beer they allow at the meals is so bad that very little can be dranke......and sometymes they are so crowded that three must lye in a bed; few people stay above two or three nights its so inconvenient...*'

And of the bath house, which she says was:

> '...about 40 foot long and about 20 or 30 foote broad being almost square...it is covered over the top, but not ceiled and there is an open place in the middle like a tunnell, which pours the cold down on your head...'[6]

This suggests that the bath roof was open to the elements and this may have been designed to let out the steam arising from the warm springs. It must certainly have been cold in the bath during the winter especially since the practice of nude bathing had become established.

The most influential 17th century physician, as far as Buxton was concerned, was Sir John Floyer of Lichfield whose book on the hot, cold and temperate baths in England, published in 1697, was devoted mainly to Buxton waters. He wrote:

> '...Their stay in the bath is an hour or more, till everyone finds themselves very cool...but no body catches cold, tho they go in naked but I think men ought to use drawers and the women shifts of linen or flannel. But custom hath taught the sexes to have separate times of bathing.'[7]

Floyer recommended a period of treatment at the Buxton bath of one week during which a diet of flesh meats and moderate drinking was prescribed. Bathing was recommended early in the morning and in the early evening, followed by the drinking of the water. Great claims were made by him regarding the success of his treatments citing successful cures for cases of *'leprosy, dropsie, lameness, pains, gravel and stone'*. Floyer's book contains a list of successful water cures carried out by himself, but much doubt must lie with his claims. Some people did undoubtedly experience relief from their symptoms and, occasionally, a complete cure, but it could be argued that this was due as much to the imposed regime of abstinence as the taking of the waters themselves.

Floyer was a friend of Dr Charles Leigh, of Oxford University, who published a large book on the natural history of Lancashire, Cheshire and the Peak in Derbyshire in 1700. Leigh

Charles Leigh, Doctor of Physick

describes experiments which he did with Floyer on the chalybeate water at Buxton and these two eminent men give us our first introduction to this iron bearing water, which we describe more fully in later chapters. Both writers refer to the bath - which we take to be the chief bath - and so we may firmly identify at least three sources of water in use at this time, the chief bath, St Anne's Well and a chalybeate well, though given Dr Jones' earlier description, there may have been other springs in use.

At the close of the seventeenth century Dr Charles Leigh reflected the growing recreation of spa bathing when he wrote of the Peak District:

> '...*She liberally affords Hot and mineral waters, for the Relief and Comfort of infirm and decrepit Mortals; so that these untractable and dispeopl'd Parts become frequented with numerous Crouds, who yearly arrive here, either through a Prospect of Ease from their Pains and Infirmities, or for the pleasing Entertainment of the Mind with new Objects, of which these parts are very prolifick...*'[8]

New Drinking Well

In 1709 Sir Thomas Delves (1632-1713) of Doddington Hall, in Cheshire, was so satisfied with his successful treatment using the Buxton waters that he decided to commemorate his cure by erecting a stone alcove over the existing drinking well dedicated to St Anne in the yard, some 25 yards north of the outer bath. In so doing he demolished the old Roman well whose remains were lost to us from that time. Delves' new well building was about twelve feet square and surrounded on its inside walls with stone benches. It had one of its four sides open to the outside with a strong bar across it to strengthen the arched roof. Inside the water rose into a stone basin in the middle of the structure.

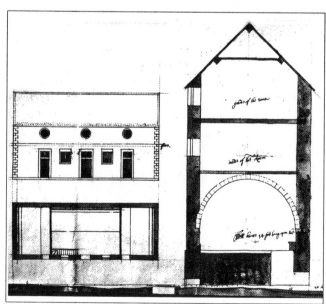
John Barker's plans of 1710/12 for new baths at the Hall

Barker's Bath

Possibly because of the poor roofing facilities at the baths, as described by Celia Fiennes, William, the second Duke of Devonshire (1673-1729) commissioned the architect John Barker of Rowsley to reconstruct the baths and other buildings adjacent to the Hall. The scheme involved the construction of a stone vault roof over the bath to protect the bathers from inclement weather. The contract was to be

Sketch of Barker's Bath as it existed in 1807, showing that the bath survived, little changed, after the 1786-88 baths remodelling by John Carr.

Buxton Bath July 1712

completed by May 1712 at a cost of £400. Barker had earlier worked at Belvoir Castle and Chatsworth upon such buildings as the stables. The facade shows the clear influence of this previous work with a row of three bulls eye windows which were a common feature in stable architecture[9].

The main inner bath (also referred to as the 'Chief' or 'Great' bath) was described by Dr Thomas Short, writing in 1734, as twenty six feet six inches long by twelve feet eight inches wide with a water depth of four foot nine inches at the lower end and four foot three inches at the head. The bath room he described as:

> '...A large stately arch room, ten yards long, five yards and a half wide, and much the same height. There is a stone bench along one end and side of it, for the bathers to dress and undress upon; between this and the bath is a walk of smooth flagstones, and at the corners of the bath, at each end, are very good stone steps or stairs to go down........At the north or lower end, is a large square hole in the foundations of the house wall, which gives vent to the water out of this into the outer bath...'[10]

Intriguingly, the Bodleian Library at Oxford possesses a sketch titled 'Buxton Bath Derbyshire, July 1712'[11], which at first sight appears to be another and perhaps stylised view of the Barker barrel-roofed inner bath. Closer examination however shows that the sketch does not have any windows on either of its long walls whereas external elevations of 1710-12 and another internal sketch of the inner bath as it appeared in 1807 clearly show three windows in its south wall. It is tempting to surmise that this sketch shows the outer bath with the two entrances on its left wall leading from the inner bath. However, as we have seen from Dr Short's description, the outer bath was still unroofed in 1734. We conclude that the Bodleian Library sketch gives a view of the Barker bath looking east.

There is some evidence of a significant extension of the Hall between 1725 and 1734. As part of this, it has been suggested by Thornes & Leach[5] that the incumbent landlord, Mr Taylor, may have built a new ladies' bath in about 1726. However this is not borne out by Short who does not mention a ladies' bath in his 1734 history though, as we have seen, he does mention the use of the outer bath by ladies. In fact it is not until 50 years later that three baths are first mentioned.

The Springs

Short's book carries a detailed description of the positioning of the town's main springs. It is not possible to vouch for the accuracy of his description, but he was in the fortunate position of being able to actually see the springs before the Crescent and baths were built over them. It is the only description we have and for that reason alone is summarised here:

1. Several warm springs arising through the floor of the (Great) Bath.

2. St Ann's Well, 32.5 yards north east of the Bath, supplied by a spring on its north side, rising through black limestone or bastard marble under a shelving stone laid for that purpose.

3. A hot and a cold spring both rising into the same receptacle in a close 20 yards south east of St Ann's Well.

4. Bingham (or Mr Leigh's) Well, 63 yards south, south east of St Ann's well.

5. Small hot spring, a little way east of Bingham Well, with an adjacent cold spring.

6. Another warm spring 34 yards east of St Ann's Well situated in the stream of the level which carries the water from the (Great) Bath.

7. Four yards further east and on the south side of this stream rise two or three other warm springs[10].

Of these springs it would seem that at least three were used for drinking, having bowls or receptacles over the spring to collect the water. One of these was Bingham Spring, which was described by Short as Mr Leigh's Well and in his contents page, though not in the main text, as St Peter's Well. Very little documented evidence for this well exists today and we are unable to ascertain whether the well was run as an organised concern or whether it was patronised on a more casual basis. Certainly, Dr Short attached some importance to this source since it is referred to in his writings in almost equal measure as the thermal spring water. Unlike the main springs the water flow from the Bingham spring varied according to the seasons, indicating that the spring probably did not originate from any great depth. The origin of the name Bingham is also unknown but the alternative name of Leigh's Well can be traced to a Mr Leigh of Lyme Hall who was a regular user of the well. By the start of the 19th century this well had ceased to be used, though it is possible that the water source was 'rediscovered' at the time of the 1851-54 rebuild of the baths. It is thought that the source of Bingham's Well is today buried under a manhole in the middle of the road separating the Pump Room and the east wing of the Crescent.

Dr Short's writings also give an insight into the medical rationale of the time with his description of how the healing waters enter the body. He wrote;

> '...*since the waters can penetrate the bather's skin, via the pores, surely it follows that they can find a passage between the fibres making up the sides of blood vessels and thus remove any obstructions which may be present and expell them...*'[10]

The premise on which the above hypothesis is based relies on the universally held belief of the time, that the skin was to some degree porous and allowed the water, together with its minerals to enter the body. Nowadays it is recognised that although absorption of liquid is, to a degree, experienced through the upper layers of the epidermis (particularly the palms of the hands and the soles of the feet), absorption of a degree likely to make sufficient difference to the functioning of the bodily organs seems very unlikely.

The 17th and 18th century medical men had very little in terms of effective drugs with which to fight infections and illnesses of all types. There was a general unawareness of the need for hygiene in the fight against bacterial infections and consequently death rates were relatively high and life spans correspondingly short. Because of the lack of specific drugs to fight disease, great emphasis was made of what they did have - sources of pure water. Bathing in and drinking of Buxton water was trumpeted as a cure for all conditions, no matter how serious. Dr Short, for example, sets out a long catalogue of the complaints which may be cured by Buxton water, in most, but not all, cases he advised both drinking and bathing.

> '...*Upon the whole, Buxton Water being warm, highly impregnated with a mineral stream, vapour or spirit, containing a most subtle and impalpable Sulphur, and being the product of Limestone; it is therefore rarefying, heating, relaxing, thinning, sweetening, and a little drying, hence it is signally beneficial, and surprisingly successful in the Gout, Rheumatism, scorbutic and arthritic Pains, wandering or fixt Pains inveterate or recent; Cramps, Convulsions, dry Asthma's without a Fever or quick Pulse, bilious Cholick, want of Appetite and Indigestion from Intemperance, hard drinking &c, Contractions, Stiffness and Lameness therefrom in any Part, Barrenness from a Constriction and idilatibility of the Fallopian Tubes and Uterus, Ringworms, Scab, Itch, for scouring off Sand, Sludge and Gravel out of the Kidneys...*'[10]*

Cure seekers of the Georgian era were not known for their personal cleanliness and many suffered from chronic skin diseases, so it is scarcely surprising that some experienced a degree of improvement in their condition since an annual or biannual bath in any type of water was likely to be beneficial!

Buxton Rivals Bath

The latter half of the eighteenth century saw a large increase in the fashion of taking the waters led in the most part by the city of Bath, with its naturally warm springs. The fifth Duke of Devonshire, who owned the Buxton baths, was concerned that the popularity of Buxton and its waters might suffer, particularly as the Royal Crescent, the New Assembly Rooms and the rebuilding of the Hot baths was undertaken at Bath between 1767 and 1777 by the architect John Wood, the younger.

At Buxton, Dr Hunter, writing in 1768[12], still describes only one bath in existence (he may not have considered a bath for the use of the poor worthy of mention, since at the time it was in a neglected condition), but by 1784 Dr Pearson describes an additional bath for the use of Ladies. This extra bath is described by Pearson as;

> '...*adjoining the old bath now appropriated to the men, called the Gentlemen's Bath...*'[13]

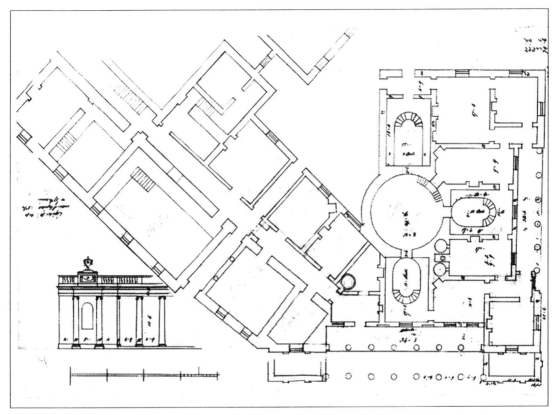

Plan of John Carr's intended new Buxton baths

It can be safely assumed that this was the large ladies' bath which existed before the addition of the four baths by John Carr, which we describe below. It is likely also that this bath would not have been open to the elements, therefore a bath building adjacent to that housing the Great Bath must have been built to accomodate it.

Despite this extra bath, the Buxton baths were inadequate for the increasing numbers seeking treatment and the duke entered into discussions with a well known northern architect, John Carr of York (1723-1807) with a view to enlarging the facilities. These discussions came to a head sometime between 1777 and 1779, and Carr was commissioned to undertake the improvements as suggested by the Duke of Devonshire. Carr was himself a sufferer of rheumatism, being greatly troubled by back and leg pain, and had taken the Buxton water cure in 1775 with some degree of relief. Carr's plans for the baths' renovation are impressive, featuring one round and three oval baths within a new building immediately to the east of the existing baths. The outside of the new baths was to boast an Ionic colonnade between two elegant Ionic pavilions with a frontage of 75 feet 6 inches in length. Unfortunately Carr had to abandon his elaborate new bath plans due to the difficulties encountered in gaining permission to build the Crescent on land to the north of the baths. The problems proved too difficult to overcome and it was eventually decided to build the Crescent on the site which had been allocated to the new baths[9].

This resulted in the building of an alternative - and probably cheaper - set of four new baths within the existing bath complex. They were designed by Carr and a detailed analysis of his building accounts suggest they were the Gentlemens' Private, the Ladies' Private, the Matlock and the Cold Bath. Work commenced with the digging of drains early in 1786. Some of the new baths were built on land previously occupied by a yard containing shops and it was necessary to pull down these shops before work could commence on the sinking of the baths.

A typical entry in Carr's building accounts details the digging out of the new gentlemen's Private Bath and the payment of four men for their work;

> '... Dec 24 1787
> *To sinking for the Gents Private Bath taking the steps out of Gents old Bath beside the pump...*
> *Willm. Eyre 6 days, 9 shillings.*
> *William Fletcher 6 days, 8 shillings.*
> *Jn Bennett 6 days, 8 shillings*
> *Jn Needam Three quarters of a day, 1 shilling...'*[14]

John Carr's building accounts of 1787 also refer to '*letting in irons at the Ladies bath to hang the chair in*', which indicates to us the early use of a chair for lowering invalids into the water. Presumably this facility was not limited to the Ladies' Bath and was also available for the gentleman bathers.

The baths were probably completed and in use by 1788 and some part of the yard still remained after the conversions, which was used as drying space for the bath towels. Although probably much renovated during the changes, the Great Bath and the Ladies' Bath remained in their original positions. The Poor Bath was removed and re-sited to the north of the new Matlock Bath and a covered way was built linking the arcades of the Square and the Crescent to the baths. Access to the baths could then be obtained through an archway in the arcade.

Dr Joseph Denman's detailed description of the complete provision in 1793 includes the four new baths, numbers 2,4,5 and 7:

1. The Gentlemen's Bath

(The original and oldest bath), 27 feet long by 17 feet wide. It was lined with polished gritstone and paved with the same and there was a pump at its south east corner. The bath had been decreased in size by a reservoir let into it to supply other baths in the complex. The reservoir was 7 feet 6 inches by 4 foot 6 inches. It had a depth of 4 feet 10 inches and a sough at its north end through the wall leading to the river which was used to empty the bath daily for cleaning purposes.

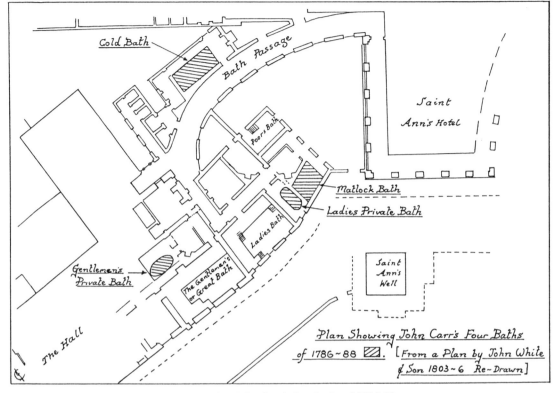

Plan showing John Carr's four baths of 1786-88

2. *The Gentlemen's Private Bath*

Situated to the south-east, and very near to the Gentlemen's Bath. This bath had an adjoining dressing room through which one passed on the way to the bath. It was oval in form, lined with grey marble and measured 10 feet 6 inches by 6 feet. The water to this bath was fed via lead pipes from the reservoir in the Gentlemen's bath. On its travel from the other bath the water lost some of its temperature and the Gentlemen's private bath was fitted with flues underneath which could raise the water temperature by many degrees. This is perhaps the earliest mention of the temperature of the water being raised artificially though, as we shall see later, the Tonic Bath also had a similar heating arrangement at about this time.

3. *The Ladies' Public Bath*

This was north of and immediately adjoining the Gentlemen's Bath, measuring 22 feet by 12 feet and made of gritstone. The water for this bath rose principally from a number of small springs in various parts of the bath floor and was supplemented by water from the main baths reservoir.

4. *The Ladies' Private Bath*
Next to the previous bath, made of grey marble and oval in shape, and measuring 11 by 4 feet. This bath was supplied with water from the main reservoir.

5. *The Matlock Bath*
This measured 11 feet 6 inches by 10 feet and was supplied by two lead pipes, one from the warm reservoir and the other from a cold (or possibly chalybeate) spring. By this method the water could be regulated to the temperature of 68°F (19.8°C) the same as that at the fashionable Matlock spring.

6. *The Poor Bath*
Measuring 8 feet square and supplied by the water overflow from the Gentlemen's Bath and made of gritstone.

All the previous six baths were provided with a 'convenient pump', which we take to mean a douche hose used by attendants to spray the bathers during treatments in the baths.

7. *The Cold Bath*
A bath situated close to the river Wye measuring 15 feet by 10 feet, probably fed from a chalybeate spring with a water temperature of 54°F (12.2° C). The river was arched over to provide flat ground for the building of this bath.

Denman further describes a tepid fountain or drinking well enclosed within the baths building, called the **Hall Well**. It was enclosed in a room opening into the corridor leading from the Hall to the Crescent[15].

The exterior of the baths building also underwent changes. If the baths exterior as designed by Barker (1712) was carried out as planned, with its two storey design and bull's eye windows, there must have been substantial changes made, as engravings from 1795 onwards show three adjoining buildings housing the baths. The building adjacent to the Hall is shown as a 3 bay, 3 storey block with windows at eaves level and the upper floors forming part of the Hall. To the side of this were two further buildings, both of two storeys. Comparing this facade with the plan of Carr's baths of 1786-88 we can suggest, with some certainty, that the three storey building housed the Great Bath and the Gentlemen's Private Bath, the middle two storey building housed the Ladies' Bath and the third building contained the Ladies' Private, the Matlock, the Poor and the Cold Baths. Denman's previous reference to a tepid fountain suggests that the Hall had direct access to the baths and it would also seem that these exterior changes took place as part of Carr's improvements.

The bath houses in 1795 to the left of the Crescent. Detailed enlargement below.

These baths were an important aspect of the new facilities at Buxton, the main feature of which was John Carr's impressive Crescent, with the accompanying stables. The Crescent was designed to provide two hotels, an assembly room and card rooms, six lodging houses and a number of shops, all under the one roof. Adjacent were the newly modernised suite of baths. Thus a whole new leisure complex was created with the Buxton air and the bathing providing an invigorating experience for the visitor. Whilst it may be said that Buxton did not reach the heights of elegance enjoyed by its rival Bath in Somerset, it could, nevertheless, offer an extensive range of entertainment. Regular balls took place in the assembly room with the card and coffee rooms in good use. The theatre in Spring Gardens, though not salubrious, offered a programme of plays in the season. Visitors would, no doubt, also take part in hunting in the Derbyshire hills or visit some of the local attractions such as Lovers Leap or Poole's Cavern. Not all visitors, it may be remarked, came only to take the water cure, or even to take the cure at all!

The Tonic Bath

A further bath was located at the bottom of Bath road (at the corner of today's Macclesfield and Burlington roads). This was the Tonic or Cold Plunge Bath which was situated on land owned by Dr Norton of Macclesfield, as recorded in the 1772 Enclosure Act. Pilkington records in 1789 that:

> '...Other springs have been discovered, and that during last summer a scheme was in agitation for erecting buildings near them for the accommodation of company...'[16]

A bath was built over these springs, measuring 30' x 12', which by 1797 had been divided to accommodate males and females separately. The temperature of this bath was nominally 63.8° F (17.7° C.) but it seemed that some difficulty was experienced in keeping the temperature stable, since the cold and tepid springs arose from various parts of the bath floor. After the separation of the bath as previously mentioned, one part of the bath was rendered capable of having its temperature raised to a comfortable level by the use of flues. The bath was fitted with a pump for the direct application of a spray of water to the bather.

Chalybeate Water

In addition to the natural thermal springs, Buxton had at least one chalybeate or iron-containing water spring. In common with most other chalybeate waters, the spring arose from a bed of shale. An early mention of this spring was made by Dr Charles Leigh in 1700, who said that a mixture of the Buxton thermal and chalybeate waters closely approximated the healing properties imparted by the waters of Bath in Somerset and of St Vincent's near Bristol.

John Carr's drinking well, situated at the foot of the slopes, opened 1783

Dr Allen, writing in 1711, mentions a chalybeate spring '*...not far off...*'[the baths][17] and Dr Short (1734) describes the same chalybeate source '*... on the north side of the brook, opposite the Hall...*' and also recommends the mixing of the thermal spring water or Bingham Well water with the chalybeate to be used as a gentle purgative. He goes on to say:

> '*...it is pretty clear as it rises, but lets fall much oker in its basin and stream, weighs pretty near the same with common water, lays the spirits in the thermometer one eighth of an inch lower than the river. It has a nauseous, rough and irony taste...*'[10]

The oker referred to here is the orange/red ferrous deposit or sinter found at the outlet of most chalybeate springs.

Dr Denman (1793) also talks of the chalybeate spring, describing its position as north of the river and immediately below the George Inn. He complains about its polluted appearance due to the recent construction of the Crescent;

> '*...Besides the tepid springs which are peculiar to Buxton, there is also a chalybeate, which rises from a bank of shale on the north side of the river, and immediately below the George inn. This spring, before the building of the Crescent, was a clear water, and much in use. Doubtless, at the time of covering the river for the purpose of erecting the Crescent with its offices, the intention was to preserve and improve this spring; as is evident from the neat little dome placed over it. By some means, however, either from the enlargement of the surface, by which it is become more exposed to the common air; or from some other cause, the water is now always in a state of decomposition, muddy and unfit for use...*'[15]

Buxton's chalybeate water emerged from the spring at a temperature of 54°F (12.2°C). It was referred to as 'mild' and was used for eye bathing and as a general tonic.

New Drinking Well

The building of the Crescent (1780-89) made it necessary to demolish the drinking well built by Delves in 1709. Under the terms of the Enclosure Act (1773-74), the Duke of Devonshire was obliged by law to provide public access to the waters and John Carr was commissioned to build a new drinking well to be sited at the foot of the slopes. For the duration of the building work a temporary well was erected at the southern corner of the Hall. The new well was completed in January 1783 with water being piped from the site of the old well which was demolished in March 1783. The new well was described by Jewitt in 1811;

> *'...A beautiful square building in the Grecian style, three sides of which have three semi-circular niches to serve as resting places for the water drinkers; the fourth, which is the entrance, is closed with a door of open iron work. This side, which is the front, is supported by two columns of the Tuscan order, and the whole building is surmounted by a beautiful urn...'*[18]

Dr George Pearson, writing in 1784 describes the interior of the new well;

> *'...the basin of the new St Anne's well is hewn out of one entire mass of gritstone, and it is covered with a massy stone of the same kind, placed in contact with the water and cemented down. An aperture is made in the side of the basin through which the water perpetually flows, as from a pump spout, at the rate of half a pint in a second of time. A neat basin of white marble is placed under the stream that flows through the aperture, for the convenience of filling glasses and other vessels with this water...'*[13]

Well Women

The Enclosure Act of 1772 decreed that St Ann's Well should be kept clean and in good repair. In order to comply with the act the Vestry (early form of local government) appointed a well woman annually after 1773/4 to look after the well and dispense the water to the public. The act appears to have formalised an already existing arrangement since an anonymous writer of 1769 records that a young female attended to dip the water. Although the annual appointment was for one woman it is likely that the total compliment was more than one, if only to cover during

MARTHA NORTON,
Aged 88
Upwards of FIFTY YEARS the attendant at the
— Buxton Wells —
Herself a proof of its salubrious Spring.'

periods of sickness.

Evidence for this assertion exists on the gravestone of Martha Brandreth at St Peter's Churchyard, Fairfield, which states that she served at the fountain of Buxton for 50 years before her death in 1795, though she was never listed as being appointed by the Vestry. The appointed woman served for one year only and names were changed often. Another well woman, the venerable Martha Norton, was elected to the post 15 times between 1775-1820, a period of 46 years if we are to assume her continuous attendance at both the Delves and the Carr well.[19]

References
1. Drayton Michael, A Chorographical Description of this Renowned Isle of Great Britain, 1622
2. Axon Ernest Op. Cit. paper 1. nd.
3. Hobbes Thomas, De Mirabilibus Pecci c.1636
4. Cotton. Charles. The Wonders of the Peake 1681 H. Brome of The Gun, St Paul's Churchyard
5. Thornes. R & Leach. J. Buxton Hall. Derbyshire Archaeological Journal. Volume CX1V. 1994.
6. Morris Christopher. The journeys of Celia Feinnes. 1949. London The Cresset Press
7. Floyer Sir John, An Enquiry into the Right Uses and Abuses of the Hot and Cold Temperate Baths in England, 1697
8. Leigh Charles. The Natural History of Lancashire, Cheshire and the Peak in Derbyshire. 1700
9. Hall. Ivan. Georgian Buxton Derbyshire Museum Service. 1984. Also Barker Deeds, BAR P666, Sheffield City Archive.
10. Short Thomas, MD. The Natural, Experimental and Medical History of the Mineral Waters of Derbyshire, Lincolnshire and Yorkshire, London 1734.
11. The Bodleian Library, Oxford, Shelfmark Ms. Top. gen.e. 61, fol. 14r
12. Hunter A. A Treatise on the nature and virtues of Buxton Waters 1768
13. Pearson. George, MD. Observations and experiments for investigating the chymical history of the tepid springs of Buxton London 1784. Vol 1.
14. Buxton Estate Accounts, Building accounts of John Carr, Devonshire Collections, Chatsworth
15. Denman Jos. MD. Observations on Buxton Water, editions of 1793 and 1801
16. Pilkington J. A View of the present state of Derbyshire 1789.
17. Allen. Dr Natural History of Mineral Waters 1711.
18. Jewitt A. History of Buxton 1811.
19. Axon Ernest FSA. Paper XV11, Early Local Government, October & November 1943.

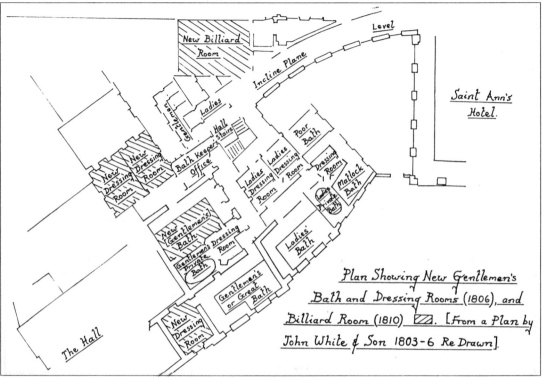

Plan showing the New Gentlemens' Bath and dressing rooms (1806) and Billiard Room (1810)
by John White and Son

The flat roof of the Hot Baths of 1818, designed by Charles Sylvester, can be seen to the right of this engraving

Chapter Three

Early 19th Century

Between 1803 and 1806 the architects John White and Son drew plans for improvements at Buxton which were, in part, intended to tidy up the area around the Crescent. The plans included the Square, designed as a group of lodging houses, and a new layout to the rear of the Crescent, as well as the new St John's Church. The overall site plan, drawn by J White jnr. in 1803 and modified in 1806, showed the proposed new developments and a number of existing buildings including the Baths[1]. The evidence from John Carr's building accounts, set out in the last chapter, leads us to conclude that the White plan shows the layout of the baths existing in 1806 but does not show any proposed new baths, since a total of seven baths are shown which, despite some small differences in orientation, almost exactly fit the description given by Denman in 1793[2].Two further pieces of evidence support this; firstly examination of the original plan shows that the proposed new developments - the Square, St John's Church - are edged in red but the baths are not so edged. Secondly, and more importantly, the Devonshire Buxton Estate accounts for 1806 show the comparatively large sum of £1273 for a new bath and alteration of others, but these changes do not appear on the plan[3]. We can be fairly certain, therefore, that the main work carried out to the baths under John White and Son was the provision of a new Gentlemen's Bath and dressing rooms, some minor renovation to others and the filling in of the Cold Bath by the river. The site of this Cold Bath was used to build a new billiard room in 1810, also designed by John White[4]. Jewitt, who published his History of Buxton in 1811, confirms these changes in his description of the baths as follows:

> '...The Baths lie to the west of St Anne's Well, and are seven in number, viz one public and two private for gentlemen; one public and one private for ladies; one, in which the water may be made to imitate that of Matlock; and one for the indiscriminate use of the poor. All except the Charity Bath have dressing rooms attached to them, furnished with every thing necessary or convenient for bathers, and servants to assist them in and out of the water...'[5]

The additional gentlemen's bath by John White and Son was called the 'new' bath and was situated to the rear of the Gentlemen's Private Bath. Dr Charles Scudamore, writing in 1820, refers to the gentlemen's 'new' bath[6] which is likely to be this same bath, since the estate accounts between 1806 and 1820 show an average yearly maintenance outlay of just over £100 but no further large expenditure[3]. It would not be unusual for the term 'new' to be applied to a bath for some years. Further confirmation is provided by Dr Carstairs, writing in 1847, who referred to this bath having been built '...*about forty years ago...*'[7]. In addition to the White's plan of 1803/6 there exists a plan entitled '*Old*

Engraving showing the Natural Baths buildings by 1820 and below, detailed enlargement.

Plan of Baths Approaches and the Square as existing prior to the alterations about 1851'[8] , which a number of writers have assumed to have been drawn in about 1851. Careful examination of this plan, however, suggests that it may have been drawn up by the Whites, certainly the style of drawing is very similar and it offers an update of the 1803/6 plan with the term 'new' applied not only to the Gentlemen's Private Bath but also to dressing rooms and the billiard room. In effect, it shows the White modifications to the Natural Baths and it could be of a much earlier date than 1851.

The Devonshire Estate took a healthy clear profit from the Natural Baths in the years between 1811 and 1820 of about £1000 per year. The year of Napoleon's defeat at the battle of Waterloo, 1815, showed particularly good profit at £1202.

The Earliest Hot Baths

In Chapter 2 we have seen that attempts were made to artificially raise the temperature of the Gentlemen's Private Bath and the Tonic Bath by the use of flues. It would seem, however, that the purpose of this was merely to raise the temperature of a colder bath to one which more closely approximated the natural mineral water temperature of 82°F (27.5°C). Whilst describing these arrangements in 1801, Denman[2] had also strongly advocated the provision of baths which could be heated to 'precise' temperatures for the treatment of such complaints as calcifications, bowel inflammation and kidney disorder. This medical recommendation must have gathered momentum and the Devonshire Estate took the decision to expand the facilities by the erection of Hot Baths in about 1816. Payments to carpenters, stone masons and plumbers working on the baths first appear in the 1817 accounts and by 20th May 1818, the baths were open for business. In that year the Estate took a clear profit of just under £250. The baths were designed by Charles Sylvester of Derby, who was something of a specialist in the installation of hot baths equipment. He was paid £86.18s.0d (£86.90) for drawings and his attendance during the erection and £32 for a warm air stove. The baths were lined with white marble and Dutch tiles, the tiles purchased from the Staffordshire firm of Josiah Wedgwood, and the total building cost was just over £1630. In 1819 the Devonshire Estate paid £615 for an additional bath with a further sum of £104 for the completion of the hot baths, and in 1820 Charles Sylvester was paid £41.8s (£41.40p) for superintending the building of the additional bath which included fitting apparatus for raising the temperature of the water[3]. The Hot Baths were fed from the overflow of the St Anne's Well and it is likely that this was supplemented with water from the Bingham spring situated at the east end of the Crescent[9].

These Hot Baths were situated at the east end of the Crescent and had direct access from the Great Hotel with a public access from a door opposite the Grove Hotel. At this time the Crescent was enclosed by a high stone wall with an entrance through an iron gate opposite the Grove Hotel, this area being known as 'Irongate'. The Hot Baths curved round from this point to join the Crescent but the building, which had a flat, lead covered roof, was masked by trees and in some contemporary engravings it is not shown. The general opinion of writers in the 1820s was that the Hot Baths building was unpretentious, but that inside it was very well equipped and included shower baths, spray pumps and dressing boxes[10].

The Natural Baths in 1820
The development of the Hot Baths, as an important additional provision, caused some changes to the Natural Baths facilities. By 1820 the Matlock Bath was no longer provided. It is possible that medical fashion had changed causing a decline in its use for treatments but a more likely reason is that it was no longer needed. By now the new Hot Baths could offer a varying degree of temperature control and the Tonic, or cold plunging, bath was available on Macclesfield road. (This Tonic bath was, in fact, likened to a Matlock Bath by some medical practitioners.) Further work on the Natural Baths took place in the years 1821/22 and a detailed examination of the accounts leads us to suggest that, in addition to the installation of ventilation stoves in the Baths building, the Matlock Bath structure was brought back into use to provide a Charity Bath for ladies. Evidence for this is that expenditure was considerably higher in those

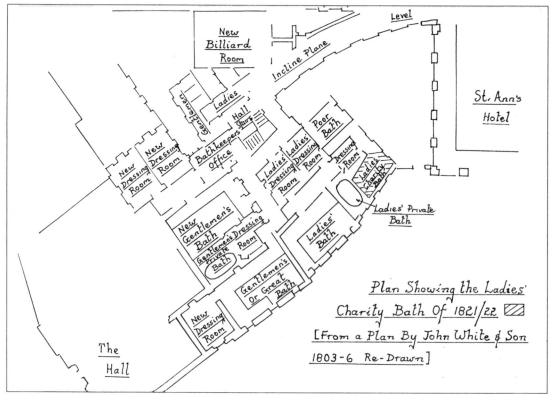

Plan showing the Ladies' Charity Bath (1821/22)

two years than in any subsequent year up to 1833 when we know there were two separate baths for male and female charity patients, each measuring 10' 8" x 10' x 4' 8" deep. The only other significant expenditure was in 1825/6 when the baths were relined with porcelain tiles supplied by Josiah Wedgwood. From 1820 to 1840 the Natural Baths returned a clear profit of about £800 pa and, apart from the work described above, the Devonshire Buxton estate spent an average of £90 yearly on maintenance[11]. A plan of the baths and Crescent area dating to about 1820 shows the extensive water management arrangements required for the provision of the Natural Baths suite. Each bath had to be fed and drained and a large sough (water channel) ran right round the outer curve of the Crescent to drain into the river at the east end[9]. It is clear also, from an engraving of about the same time, that the external facade had been tidied up sometime between 1805 and 1820, possibly as part of the John White & Son work. The engraving shows the building housing the Great Bath and other gentlemen's baths having four storeys and its roof line raised to the same level as the Hall. The other baths are housed in a neat two bay, two story building adjacent.

Chalybeate spring

Dr Denman, in the second edition of his book (1801), noted that the chalybeate spring, situated near the George Inn, was still contaminated, muddy and unfit for use, despite the fact that it was protected by a small dome or arch. It was still out of use in 1811 when Jewitt observed that the water, '*...preserved in a gritstone basin arched over...*' had become shamefully neglected and was totally unfit for use. This suggests that the water was unavailable for at least 30 years. In 1819, however, the well was rebuilt at a cost of £9.18s.1d. [£9.90.] and it was in use again from that time, being maintained by the Devonshire Buxton Estate.

It is likely that this rebuilding included routing the water through a sculpted lion's mouth. Guide books from 1820 show engravings of this 'lion's mouth' well and Dr Robertson, writing in 1838, said that the chalybeate was commonly referred to in the town as 'lion's mouth water'[12/13]. As an iron bearing water it was considered weak but very pure and its temperature was 54°F (12.1°C). It was considered by Dr Robertson as a useful tonic for the eyes but also effective for 'indolent swelling' of the joints when poured from a spouted jug over the affected joints two or three times a day. The medical practitioner, TJ Page, who was surgeon to the Buxton Bath Charity in the 1840s, cites the successful use of the chalybeate in the case of a young lady with 'gastrodynia' (pain in the stomach). He prescribed two half pints to be taken each day and said that, within a fortnight, she was well and had no return of the ailment[14]. So here we see examples of the chalybeate water being prescribed as both an internal and external treatment.

After 1845, the chalybeate well in George Street was covered with an 'umbrella like' structure which was removed in 1858 and placed in the Crescent to provide a

The chalybeate spring or 'Lion's Mouth Well'

cover for for the town band[15]. By 1853 water from the chalybeate well had been piped into a new well room provided as part of the newly designed Natural Baths building.

Tonic or Cold Plunge Bath

The Tonic or Cold Plunge Bath referred to in the last chapter, owned by Dr Norton, was described by Jewitt (1811) in somewhat disparaging terms. He said that there were both warm and cold springs here but that, due to mismanagement, these could never be properly separated and that the temperature was, therefore, 64°F (17.6° C). He suggests that the efforts made by Dr Norton to raise the temperature by means of flues was not only unsuccessful, but was an attempt to deceive the public by substituting an artificial for a natural bath. This is, perhaps, being a little hard on Dr Norton, since his heating arrangements were similar to those employed in the Gentlemen's Private Bath, as we have seen in Chapter 2.

The Tonic Bath was cold, though there is a lack of consistency in the measurement of its temperature by writers in the early nineteenth century, with recordings varying between 60° F and 68° F (15.4°C and 20°C). Being a natural cold spring, it is likely that the temperature would vary with the seasons. It was compared with the tepid springs at Matlock which were said to measure 68°F (20°C) on average.

The bath was described in 1819 as having water at a temperature of 60°F (15.4°C) and though it had previously been divided into separate sections for ladies and gentlemen, by that time it was one single bath but with a floor of two different depths[6]. In 1823 the bath was open but not much used and by 1835 it was being run by Mr William Moore. A guide book of 1842 suggested that, whilst the accommodation offered at this bath was perfect and the terms moderate, nevertheless it was not much frequented since most people came to Buxton for the natural mineral waters and their medicinal properties[16].

By 1847 the Tonic Bath was closed but it was again open in 1852 with William Boam as the bath keeper[17]. In November 1860 the bath and bathhouse were offered for sale by auction[18] and from 1861 there is reference to this bath in the Devonshire Buxton accounts when a new drain was laid at a cost of just over £79 and William Boam paid £16 in rent. It is conceivably possible that the Devonshire Buxton Estate had acquired the bath, for between 1862 and 1864 the estate paid for substantial repairs. The nature of the work suggests that the bath was re-excavated or enlarged, properly drained and covered with stonework and an iron roof. A new road to the bath was laid and the total cost was just under £500 which included the architect Henry Currey's fee. In 1865 an income statement for the Tonic Bath appeared in the Estate accounts for the first time at £4.16s.0d (£4.80) and £16 was spent on repairs. In 1866 the income was £11.16s.0d (£11.80) and £24 was spent on repairs, mainly plumbing. In 1867 the income was not separately identified but the bath was only open for a short time, for which James Boam, who was the attendant at the Natural Baths, was paid a small amount for attendance and washing at the Tonic Bath. A letter of complaint to the Buxton Advertiser in August 1867 confirms that the Tonic Bath was closed[15].

It would seem that the Devonshire Buxton Estate had directly managed the bath for a short time but found it ran at a loss. However between 1868 and 1870 the Estate paid for further substantial work to be carried out on the bath and the house adjoining (probably Bath House) at a cost of just under £485 which included '...*new metal piping and setting the bath in order...*' In 1869 William Boam, who had paid £16 per year rent for the Tonic Bath continuously from 1861, died and from Michaelmas (September 29th) of that year, Thomas Woodruff took on the lease, though at the considerably increased rent of £90.10s 0d (£90.50). Woodruff probably ran the bath as a private concern until 1881, though it was described as 'disused' on the 1878 survey plan. In 1882 the lease was taken by Thomas and MB Wilson but, although the accounts show that the '...*Tonic Bath and house were given up from Ladyday 1881...*' (March 25th), Woodruff continued to pay a rent of £40 pa, certainly until 1891, when records of the Estate accounts cease. The Wilsons paid a rent of £50 during this time[19]. As far as we can ascertain the Tonic Bath continued to operate, though we are not sure as to the nature of the bathing arrangements. In 1889 it was referred to by name in a local guide, though other guides of 1891 and 1894 refer to it as a tepid swimming bath and a Buxton Guide of 1896 describes '...*the swimming bath at the end of Broad Walk is large and well kept and is supplied with limestone water at 60°F...'*[20].

The Tonic Baths about 1947

The bath operated as a swimming facility well into the 20th century and it was, in its later years, covered by a semi-cylindrical structure. Buxtonians who swam there remember the coldness of the water and the large cast iron pipes round the edge of the bath which were formerly used for heating. According to the Buxton Advertiser of July 1946, the bath was acquired by the Spa Hotel, who carried out some renovations and opened it on a club membership basis. It is not known how long this arrangement continued but the site was built upon in the late 1950s and nothing now remains of the bath.

St Anne's Well Women

The well designed by John Carr was in use throughout the first half of the nineteenth century and was staffed by well women who were appointed annually at a meeting of the Vestry, which was the early form of local government. In 1818 the Vestry appointed Peggy Brandreth and set out duties for her and the other women. These included helping the poor women in the Charity Bath, cleaning out the bath and drying mats, bathing gowns and towels. In 1822 there were three well women and, since they were not paid but relied on tips for income, we cannot be certain whether they fulfilled the duties set out. It is perhaps not surprising that in 1840 the Buxton Bath Charity resolved to appoint their own female Charity Bath attendant. The well women supplemented their income by selling articles at the well, though this was stopped in 1842. As we shall see later, the appointment of well women continued into the latter part of the nineteenth century[21].

The Early Victorian Natural Baths

The provision in the Natural Baths remained largely the same from the mid 1820s to the major rebuilding in the early 1850s. Writing in 1838, Dr WH Robertson, who was to become Buxton's best known medical specialist, described the Natural Baths as follows:

> '...*The natural baths, exclusive to those devoted to the use of the patients of the Buxton Bath Charity are five in number, respectively called "The Ladies' Public Bath" - "The Ladies' Private Bath" - "The Gentlemen's Public Bath" - "The Gentlemen's Large Private Bath" - and "The Gentlemen's Small Private Bath". Of these the oldest is the Gentlemen's Public Bath. It is lined with smooth stone. Through interstitial crevices, purposely left between the stones which form the floor of this bath, the water enters from the spring itself. The water in this bath is four feet nine inches deep. The length of the bath is rather more than 25 feet, and it is about 12½ feet wide. The temperature of the water in the bath is within a small fraction of 82 degrees by Fahrenheit's thermometer.*
>
> *From this bath, at its south western-corner, a portion of the water, as it comes through the natural crevices of the limestone, is cut off and collected in a reservoir, from which three of the other baths are supplied by pipes, which are laid with such jealous care, that the water only loses one degree of heat in its passage from the reservoir to any of the baths supplied from it. The Gentlemen's small private bath is of an oval shape. The long diameter of it is 13½ feet, the short diameter 6 feet. The temperature of the water in this bath is within a fraction of 81½ degrees. The bath is lined with white porcelain. The Gentlemen's large private bath is of an oblong square shape. Its length is 21 feet, its breadth more than 10½ feet. The bath is lined with white porcelain. The depth of the water in this bath and in the Gentlemen's small private bath is 4 feet 8 inches. The Ladies' public bath is an oblong square. Its length is 21 feet, its breadth 12 feet. The depth of water in the bath is 4 feet 6 inches. It is lined with smooth stone. The Ladies' private bath is 12 feet long, and 4½ feet wide. The depth of water is 4 feet 6 inches. It is lined with white porcelain. All these baths are provided with forcing-pumps, by which the water may be directed against any affected part with very considerable force. Proper dressing rooms, well aired, are attached to the several baths...*'[13].

These five baths for paying patients and the two Charity Baths were unchanged when described by Dr Carstairs in 1847. He referred to the Gentlemen's Private Bath as the 'Duke's Bath' and the Gentlemen's Large Private Bath (still being described in 1839 as the 'New Bath') as the 'Gentlemens' Two Shilling Bath'. He also described the Charity Baths, one for men and one for women, as being in a yard adjoining the Ladies' Bath. The yard referred to was an open space between the baths and the Crescent through which access to the Charity Baths was gained[7].

The water for drinking was dispensed from St Anne's Well, the Grecian style building designed by Carr and situated in the Crescent, opposite the Natural Baths. Dr.Robertson observed that the effects of the Buxton waters when taken internally were in some degree the same as those produced when used as a bath. He set out the regime for taking the water as follows:

> *'...Half a pint is the quantity commonly taken at once. It is usual to take the first dose before breakfast and the remainder during the forenoon. It is justly considered to be most improper to drink the waters shortly before going into the bath....It is seldom necessary to take more than a pint and a half of these waters every day but cases do occasionally occur in which it is found to be by no means wise to restrict the patient to the use of this quantity of the waters, but in which considerably more, and probably twice this quantity, is taken with advantage...'13*

Victorian Water Treatments

The bathing treatments advocated by Dr Scudamore in the late 1830s centred around immersion in the baths for specific periods of time and the use of pumps to spray affected parts of the body with varying degrees of force. Scudamore suggested that patients resorting to Buxton were suffering usually, but not exclusively, from gout or rheumatism, and he advocated medication and other forms of treatment in conjunction with the water regime. A recent medical thesis has summarised the types of treatment prescribed by Scudamore from an extensive number of case histories in his book published in 1839.

> *'...For rheumatism and gout it was recommended that an antiphologistic (poultice) be applied before bathing and, for stubborn attacks, a technique of blistering was used to increase the blood supply to the specific area and to concentrate the body's own curative powers. The blister was formed by applying a caustic substance and the cuticle was removed on vestication (ie. the* superficial skin was removed after the blister had formed) *when two grains of acetate of morphia (highly soluble) were then rubbed into the cutis.* (the underlying skin). *This, not surprisingly, led to 48 pain free hours. Leeches were also applied to local areas of inflammation then warm water pumped over the area followed by shampooing (massage). Medication in the form of colchium (a garden bulb, used until recently in the treatment of gout) or quinine was used to reduce fever. Quinine was also used for neuralgia and morphine was given for pain relief. If the patient did not return to full vigour a tonic, in the form of liquor arsenalis might be offered, as Sir Charles Scudamore said '...in particular forms of disease we can avail ourselves of this powerful mineral tonic without fear of injury. Yet I must observe it is not a medicine to be given on common occasions nor ever without a careful watching of its effects..'*
>
> *Arsenic was also used in skin complaints and sasparilla doubled as a treatment for both chronic rheumatism and skin disease.*
>
> *Sciatica was treated by having mercury rubbed into the affected part to the extent of causing ptyalism (meaning excessive salivation, a symptom of early mercury poisoning). Mercury was chiefly used to treat syphillis. Carbonate of iron (a tonic) was taken by day and as much 'black drop' with acetate of morphia and camphor as necessary for sleep and tranquility at night. Black drop is presumed to be liquorice water* (though tar water was also used as a curative from the 18th century).
>
> *Stomach and liver troubles were treated with bark saline in effervescence with free doses of the black drop or Brandish's alkaline (probably a local apothecary) and disulphate of quinine. Infections of the the respiratory tract were dealt with by application of acetate of conium liniment to sedate the respiratory centre and having analgesic properties to soothe any pain. (this treatment is a compound of Hemlock which causes death by asphyxiation) Liniments were also used on painful joints, namely, soap liniment, belladonna (which is poisonous if applied to broken skin) and veratia which had analgesic properties...'22.*

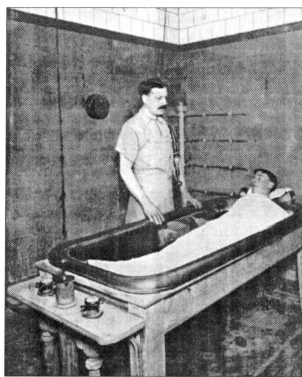

Victorian Water Treatments
Left: Buxton massage and douche
Below: Vapour bath at Buxton

Scudamore used these treatments in conjunction with various forms of water bathing, douche and massage. He advised that the baths should be emptied and refilled every day and that the utmost cleanliness should be observed in all the bathing arrangements[6]. The surgeon T J Page offered five rules of bathing:

> '...*First go into the Bath about the middle of the day.*
> *Second - to go into the Bath when the body is warm*
> *Third - to go in with the feet first*
> *Fourth - to remain in the water FIRST but a very short time*
> *Fifth - To bathe on alternate days, or to miss every third day...*'[14]

The term 'Public' and 'Private' is frequently used to describe baths and it may be helpful to explain the distinction. As far as we can ascertain a 'Private' bath would be used by a single patient at any one time, whereas a 'Public' bath would be used by several patients together. As medical techniques developed beyond simple bathing and rudimentary massage and douche sprays, it was recognised that a large expanse of water was not required for single patient treatment and the size of 'Private' baths became smaller.

The Hot Baths in the early 1840s

The Hot Baths produced a clear profit of about £300 a year from the time they were built into the 1840s and expenditure on maintenance averaged £60 pa. The baths were fed from the natural mineral springs into a cistern enclosed within a larger cistern and, between the two, steam was circulated to heat the water to a temperature of about 95°F (35°C). The most expensive operating outlay was for coal and the expenditure on the boiler also tended to be high, so clearly the provision of hot baths was quite a costly operation.

But the baths were popular and by 1840 the facilities had been doubled to two Baths for Gentlemen and two for Ladies, with a vapour and shower bath for each. The expansion may have taken place in 1836/7 when there was increased expenditure including the provision of a new office.

T J Page, writing in 1843, made special mention of the vapour and shower baths at Buxton. He suggested that the vapour (or steam) bath was an effective treatment for gout, rheumatism, fever, liver complaints and incipient consumption, amongst other complaints and that the bathing regime might be from 20 to 30 minutes in a bath of between 120°F to 130°F (48.5°-55°C). He observed that shower baths were perhaps the most unexceptionable mode of bathing but nevertheless, went on to say '...*When there is a natural determination of blood to the head, I know no means so generally effectual in restoring the balance of circulation as a course of shower bathing...*'[14].

T J Page also mentioned the operation of 'shampooing' as part of the water treatment and recommended Mr Joseph Miller of the Market Place, Buxton as a skilful

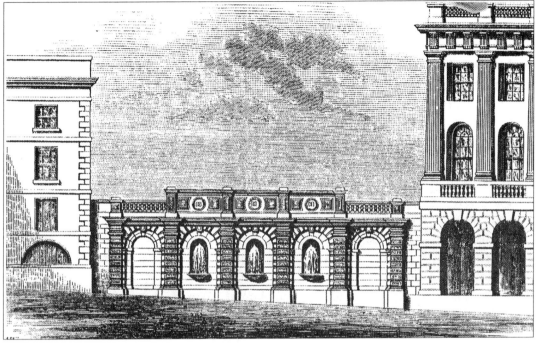

The Natural baths 1854

The Hot Baths 1854

practitioner in the art of 'shampooing and galvanizing'. Miller described himself as an 'anatomical shampooer' and this is, of course, massage (though the word had yet to come into common parlance). By 1842 there were a number of such shampooers, some resident and some who visited the town in the season. As demand grew, these medical assistants became resident in Buxton and worked in association with the doctors giving hot air, shower and vapour baths, as well as various forms of shampoo or massage.

The major rebuild of the Baths 1851-1854

The Great Exhibition of 1851 in Hyde Park clearly showed the progress which Britain had made in innovation and industry in the 19th century, and it was to preface the production of widespread wealth through new and expanded industries. Buxton had enjoyed steady, if not spectacular, growth through the first half of the century, exemplified by the extension of the bathing arrangements, but the second half of the century was to see the town really expand as an inland spa. Between 1849 and 1852 the Royal Hotel was built, the largest and most important building since the Square. The Royal, designed by the Sheffield architect Samuel Worth, and built for the solicitor Andrew Brittlebank, was an early piece of private development in the town. It was to be followed by the Quadrant, built as individual private investments between 1853 and 1864 but retaining the same architectural style to the front curved facade[15].

The decision to invest in a complete rebuild of the Hot and Natural Baths was probably taken in 1851 and Joseph Paxton, designer of the Great Exhibition's Crystal Palace and close confidante of the 6th Duke of Devonshire, may well have had more than a passing interest in this development at Buxton. The remodelling of the Baths was carried out to the designs of Henry Currey, the Duke of Devonshire's architect. The Natural Baths old buildings were pulled down in early 1852 and by April work was progressing rapidly. The designs for the external facade of the two buildings were very different, but the construction of the roofs at both the Hot and Natural Baths involved the same glass 'ridge and furrow' principle.

The principle contractors were London firms, with Sanders & Woolcott responsible for the main contract, William Jeakes of Bloomsbury for the major plumbing and Mr Riddell carrying out the plastering of the Hot Wing. The ironwork to the Hot Wing was, however, provided by John Walker of York. The Builder magazine of August 20th 1853 carried the following description:

> '...The Baths consist of two distinct buildings...both being approached under cover (a point of much importance for invalids)...one is called the "natural wing" from the water being used there at its natural temperature; the other the "hot wing" where the temperature is artificially raised to any required extent. The tepid springs issue from the limestone rocks immediately under the site of the natural wing, and some of the baths are supplied through perforations in the marble bottoms which are laid hollow over the rock. The baths are built at such a level that the height to which the springs rise forms the required depth. A reservoir

is formed at the principal source and the water flows continuously from there to the whole range of baths. The water is also led from the same service to a large reservoir under the hot wing to supply that building but here the water has to be pumped up into tanks to supply the different baths. It was deemed of great importance to have the natural wing built immediately over the springs, so that the gases in the water might escape as little as possible. The ground is of an irregular shape, and part of the baths are formed in the lower storey of the Old Hall Hotel...'

'...Wide corridors...are sufficiently commodious to serve as waiting rooms. Two dressing rooms are provided to each private bath which gives an opportunity of working them more expeditiously. Douche, shower, vapour and commodious charity baths for both sexes are provided in each wing with distinct entrances. A room for drinking the tepid waters from St Anne's Well and another for drinking a strong chalybeate, brought from a hill adjoining, are provided in the same building.

The natural wing, from the character of the site, exhibits only one facade, executed in the stone of the neighbourhood of a rich warm colour, and there being no windows or doors in it, three fountains in fluted niches are introduced to give life to the elevation. The hot wing, which exhibits two considerable facades, is constructed in iron and glass, producing a variety, and enabling the architect to give the utmost degree of lightness and cheerfulness to the interior. The roofs are formed on the "ridge and furrow" principle in 9 and 10 feet spans...the whole is glazed with Hartley's 'rough plate'...sun blinds are provided internally...the baths are lined with patent glazed porcelain bricks...the bottoms are formed with veined Sicilian marble and the whole of the private and douche baths in the hot wing are formed with similar marble...the natural wing is warmed by means of hot water, and the hot wing by steam from the boilers...'[23]

This is a detailed account from which we learn some important points. The Baths were clearly completed quite quickly, substantially between April 1852 and August 1853. The Devonshire Buxton accounts indicate that the baths remained open for business during the rebuild and there is a note in the 1853 accounts which refers to the extra expense incurred in keeping both the old and the new Hot Baths open during the season.

The article describes how the water was routed to the Hot Baths and that a pump was required to raise it to the level required. This, as we shall see, was an expensive process, expenditure on coal being one of the greatest operating costs. The Builder article also states quite clearly that the roofing of both Baths was on the glazed 'ridge and furrow' principle. The use of ridge and furrow roofing was comparatively new in 1851, having been invented by Joseph Paxton in the early 1830s as part of his design for conservatories.

There is a school of thought which suggests that Paxton may have had some influence in the design of the Hot Baths in that the ridge and furrow roof and glazed sides were descendants of the Lily House which he designed at Chatsworth in 1849/50. Henry Currey had worked with Paxton on the Prince's Park, Liverpool in 1843, and when Currey designed the Long Conservatory at Chiswick, in 1850, he consulted Paxton at the wish of the Duke of Devonshire[24]. In the early 1850s Paxton designed the layout of the Park at Buxton, and was probably responsible for modification to the slopes and for the layout of Corbar Woods, which were maintained by the Chatsworth

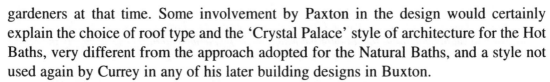

gardeners at that time. Some involvement by Paxton in the design would certainly explain the choice of roof type and the 'Crystal Palace' style of architecture for the Hot Baths, very different from the approach adopted for the Natural Baths, and a style not used again by Currey in any of his later building designs in Buxton.

The Natural Baths now offered two public and two private baths for men, effectively the original or Great Bath, which had always been a public bath, and the 1806 White Bath, which had previously been described as a private bath, formed the public bath provision. The ladies' accommodation was one public and two private baths. Two well rooms for drinking purposes were provided, one for the natural mineral water and the other for chalybeate water. The baths were entered from corridors off the Crescent colonnade in between the two well rooms. There were also two Charity Baths, one each for male and female and these were entered from a yard at the back of the building. The Hot Baths offered one public and four private baths for men and the same for women and a public cold plunge bath. There were also two baths each for male and female charity patients, which were entered from the rear of the building. Both sets of baths contained douche closets, dressing rooms and other facilities required for medical bathing.

Amongst the many items of furniture and equipment for the Baths were cocoa matting made at the New Bailey Prison, Salford, a washing machine costing £7.7s.0d (£7.35) and a patent mangle which cost £15.15s.0d. (£15.75). In 1852 Dr Lyon Playfair was asked to carry out an analysis of the water and this was published and distributed by post to more than 3500 addresses as part of the publicity for the baths.

The new baths were a great success and featured in an article, with an engraving, in the Illustrated London News of August 1854[25]. In the same year Dr Robertson, Buxton's foremost authority on water treatment, published the first edition of his Buxton Guide, in which he gave a full description of the baths and medical treatments[26].

From the opening of the new baths to 1860 the Devonshire Buxton Estate took a clear profit on their operation of about £1800 per annum, the best year being 1856 when a clear profit of £2187 was earned. During this time the bathman was paid £78 and the bathwoman £40 a year.

The remodelling of the water facilities included the dismantling of the old St.Anne's Well designed by Carr, though the urn which surmounted it was saved and can now be seen on the Devonshire Royal Hospital. The drinking well became part of the Natural Baths complex and the well women continued to dispense the water, for which they received a gratuity. In 1872 they were allowed to put up a notice saying that they were supported by voluntary contribution. In 1873 there were six well women but they ceased to be appointed after 1875. The requirements of the Enclosure Act meant that a separate free supply of the waters had to be made available to the public. This was complied with in 1855 when the Buxton Estate paid £132 for the erection of a

Hot Bath with crane

Needle Bath

Hot Bath with douche

double pump which dispensed natural tepid water from one side and cold from the other.

Bathing Medicine

The range of treatments included bathing programmes, (often associated with dietary regimes), douches or sprays on affected parts of the body (including the use of double-action force pumps) and also massage. John Pearson, a consulting surgeon at the Devonshire Hospital set out reports of cases of treatment to charity patients in a booklet in 1861, of which the following are typical:

> *CASE LXXXII*
> *M.B. Age 39, a Charwoman. August 18th 1860. Had Rheumatic Fever in January. Has now pain in all her joints - bowels costive - tongue white - pulse quick and feeble - slight cough - has palpitation sometimes when lying down. Ordered dose of physic - 3 warm baths.*
> *August 25th. Less pain - feels better - continue warm baths.*
> *September 1st. Bowels costive - physic - continue warm baths.*
> *September 8th. Discharged. Much relieved*
> *CASE LXXXV*
> *P.C. age 53, a Weighing Clerk. August 18th 1860.*
> *This man was here in June and July; commenced being worse after getting home, and could not work. Ordered warm baths.*
> *September 1st. Much better. Ordered natural baths and douche. Remained until 26th, and went home Cured*[27].

During the major rebuild of the Natural Baths, the medical practitioners had insisted that the design should allow for the natural mineral water to be used right over the spring sources. Dr Robertson was a keen advocate of this, arguing that the effect of the water bubbling up through the floor of the bath was of itself extremely beneficial, and that baths sited away from the spring source (thus of a lesser temperature than the normal 82°F (27.5°C) were much less effective in their treatment. Not all doctors held this view. Dr Carstairs observed that the Charity Baths were some distance from the spring source and thus of a slightly lower temperature yet great claims were made for the cure rate of charity patients. Dr Robertson maintained his stance, however, and as we shall see later, this had a particular effect on the siting of the new Charity Baths in 1876. He advanced a very clever argument in respect of the Hot Baths, saying that if you took water at a natural temperature of, say 50°F (10° C) and heated it to 95°F (34.6° C) you would materially affect the characteristics of that water, whereas taking Buxton mineral water at 82°F(27.5°C) required only a small amount of additional heat and this would be less likely to affect the medicinal properties of the water.

Dr Robertson wrote extensively on the effects of the Buxton natural mineral water. He asserted that the Buxton baths were most effective in cases of rheumatism, gout, neuralgia and certain forms of spinal, uterine and dyspeptic affections. He advised that no invalid should come to take the baths without the express advice and sanction of their usual medical attendant and furthermore that '...*medical men cannot be made too fully cognizant of the stimulating and alternative character of these mineral waters...*'

Robertson was careful also to protect his specialised knowledge, indicating that only a medical person who had been closely associated with the use of such waters in medical treatment over a period of time could properly advise on treatments, therefore the patient should always use the waters under the direction of a medical man resident in Buxton. He was unequivocal in this advice saying:

> '...*It is my duty to state this...and to urge it upon public attention; and the seniority of my position enables me to do this with a less chance of misconstruction, and justifies me in doing so...*'[28]

Dr W H Robertson built a formidable medical reputation in Buxton over 60 years from 1837.

The Turkish Bath

By 1864 some changes had been made to the Hot Baths, though the Natural Baths remained much the same as in 1854. In the Hot Baths, the Gentlemen's Large Hot Public Bath had been converted to private baths. The Cold Swimming Bath had been closed and the accommodation used as a billiard room. These changes took place in 1860 at a cost of £161. The old billiard room was converted into a reading room which formed part of the business of J C Bates, the proprietor of the Buxton Advertiser, whose offices were in the Hot Baths Colonnade by 1864.

The most important change was the introduction of Turkish, or Hot Air Bath department into the Hot Baths. The building work was carried out in 1861 and the baths were situated on the eastern side, behind the former cold swimming bath.The building cost was £1082 and the architect, Henry Currey, was paid a fee of £61.12s.0d [£61.60] for their design.

The Devonshire Buxton Estate were taking an income from the Turkish Baths from August of 1861 though it was very modest and the venture was short lived. In 1863 the manager, Mr James Seeley left and by June 1865 the baths had been closed. The Turkish Baths simply did not pay, in fact the income derived was not even enough to cover the operating costs and it would seem that this form of bath was not popular in the 1860s.

Hot Bath and Devonshire Colonnades

Within just a few years of opening, it was recognised that the Hot Baths were a prime site for shops. In 1863 storerooms at the front of the building were converted into two shops, one of which was occupied by John Milligan, the draper, and the other by Thomas Woodfuff who ran a spa museum. We have already mentioned J C Bates and the Buxton Advertiser office and by 1864 there were five other shops in the newly

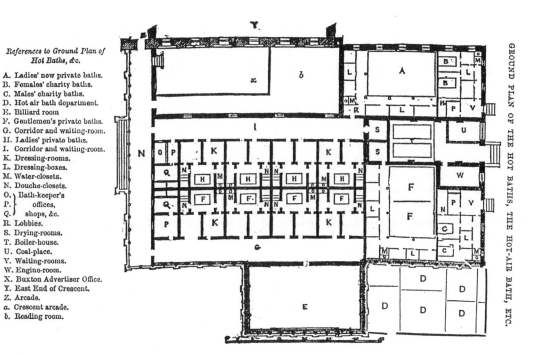

References to Ground Plan of Hot Baths, &c.

A. Ladies' new private baths.
B. Females' charity baths.
C. Males' charity baths.
D. Hot air bath department.
E. Billiard room
F. Gentlemen's private baths.
G. Corridor and waiting-room.
H. Ladies' private baths.
I. Corridor and waiting-room.
K. Dressing-rooms.
L. Dressing-boxes.
M. Water-closets.
N. Douche-closets.
O. ⎫ Bath-keeper's
P. ⎬ offices,
Q. ⎭ shops, &c.
R. Lobbies.
S. Drying-rooms.
T. Boiler-house.
U. Coal-place.
V. Waiting-rooms.
W. Engine-room.
X. Buxton Advertiser Office.
Y. East End of Crescent.
Z. Arcade.
a. Crescent arcade.
b. Reading room.

GROUND PLAN OF THE HOT BATHS, THE HOT-AIR BATH, ETC.

Plan of the Hot Baths 1864 showing the Turkish or Hot Air Baths (marked 'D')

Devonshire Colonnade Buxton

The Hot baths and Devonshire Colonnade1866

formed 'Hot Bath Colonnade', including J W Potter, hosier, and W Oram, fruiterer and poulterer. By 1866 the whole east side of the Hot Baths had been turned into shops to form a further new shopping amenity called the Devonshire Colonnade and the Baths building then housed five shops in the Hot Bath Colonnade and six in the Devonshire Colonnade.

New Roofs to the Baths

Despite the changes to the Hot Baths, no significant modifications were made to the Natural Baths until the re-roofing of 1865/6. The glass ridge and furrow roofing had proved to be uncomfortably hot in summer and excessively cold in winter, as well as being prone to leaking. The glass was replaced with slates and skylights by a Manchester contractor, Robert Carlyle, on a contract worth £1373 over two years. The architect for the work was Henry Currey though local supervision was provided by the surveyor to the Buxton Estate, Robert Rippon Duke.

The contract did not run particularly smoothly and R R Duke entered into much correspondence with Robert Carlyle and with the Duke of Devonshire's Buxton Agent, George Drewry. At one point R R Duke tried to introduce local plumbers onto the job because the contractors were not getting on with the work to his satisfaction. It may be for this reason that similar re-roofing of the Hot Baths, which took place in 1868/9 was carried out by local tradesmen, including the plumbing firm of Joseph Broomhead of Terrace Road. The re-roofing work on the Hot Baths cost more than that at the Natural Baths, though it also included widening the colonnade and other maintenance.

By 1870 the Baths were producing a combined income in excess of £5500 pa and showing a net profit of between £3500 and £4500 pa, depending upon cost of maintenance and improvements. Typically, around 59,000 baths would be taken in the year. In 1869/70 considerable work was undertaken at the Baths to increase the supply of water to both buildings. Additional reserve tanks were fitted at the Hot Baths and new connections made to the Natural building. The main contractor for the work was Edward Frith, who had done other water engineering work for Buxton. The work, which also included a new boiler and heating tank at the Hot Baths, cost more than £1000 and was supervised by the estate surveyor, Robert R Duke.

New Charity Baths

From 1870 profit on the baths continued to grow steadily and by 1875 a net profit of more than £5000 was achieved. Buxton was now a thriving spa with the baths supporting a wide range of services from bath chair men to laundries and a comprehensive range of hotels and lodging houses to suit all tastes and pockets.

The Devonshire Buxton Estate was deriving a good income from the baths and the agent, George Drewry, was obviously keen to enhance their commercial viability, hence the investments made on the Hot Baths and the attempts in the early 1870s to increase the flow of water.

For some time the agent had been attempting to find alternative bathing accommodation for the Charity patients, so that their not inconsiderable facilities could be converted to provide additional accommodation for paying patients. He was concerned that the Baths were becoming overcrowded (a fact also referred to in the Buxton Advertiser) and wanted the Charity Baths to be removed to the Devonshire Hospital. Discussion and argument over this issue continued for four or five years and several schemes were put up, including work by Henry Currey and the local architect Robert Rippon Duke. The main sticking point was with Dr Robertson's firmly held view that the further away the bath was sited from the springs, the less the efficacy of the water. He felt that the Devonshire Hospital was too far away to house the baths. By late 1875 a neat compromise solution had been proposed by R R Duke, who became the architect for new Charity Baths. He sited one new Natural Bath for charity patients behind the Old Hall Hotel, partly under the road servicing the Square, and new Charity Hot Baths, two each for men and women, in George Street. These baths were fed from the overflow of the Gentlemen's Two Shilling (Large Public) and the Ladies Large Public Baths[15].

With the Charity Baths building underway, no time was lost to expand the facilities in the Hot and Natural Baths and work was already progressing in October 1875. The trend towards provision of smaller private baths was continued in this refurbishment with the Hot Baths being composed entirely of Private Baths. Separate corridors led to ranges of 10 private baths each for ladies and gentlemen. Each bath was equipped with a dressing room, douche equipment and shower bath. The individual baths were shallow, and could be prepared to any temperature required.

The Natural Baths retained the three large Public Baths as follows: firstly the original Public Bath (formerly the Great Bath, but much modified over the years) was now called the Two Shilling Bath, and measured 26' x 18'. Secondly the Gentlemen's No 2 Bath, which had previously been called the Two Shilling Bath was now demoted to the One Shilling Bath, measuring 27' x 15'. Thirdly the Ladies' Public Bath. In addition the Natural Baths now had four Private Baths for ladies and five for gentlemen each measuring 11' x 5' together with the usual dressing rooms, douche apparatus and shower baths.

The work also included the relaying of the marble floors to the Gentlemen's Public Baths and the provision of additional douche apparatus. The main contractors for this work were J Barnsley & Sons, with a firm called Haden & Co carrying out the engineering work. The total contract, paid over the years 1875-7 was £7235. Henry Currey was paid the usual 5% architect's fee.

Consolidation

From the major rebuild of 1853, we have seen a continuing, and not inconsiderable, capital expenditure on the Hot and Natural Baths up to the mid 1870s and we might expect to look for an extended period beyond this when the Buxton Estate would seek to capitalise on its investment. This appears to be the case between 1877 and 1891, after which the detailed accounts cease to be available. Gross income in those years approached £6500 and clear profit averaged £4000. Outgoings were limited in the main to operating expenses and modest maintenance costs, though at the Hot Baths the expenditure on coal was one of the highest of the operating costs and fairly regular payments were made for boiler maintenance and refurbishment.

During this time however, techniques of hydrotherapy were advancing rapidly, pushed on by the hydropathic movement where treatments were developed, using ordinary water, in hotels called hydros. By 1890 Buxton had several of these establishments including Malvern House on Hartington Road, Clarendon House on Manchester Road, Haddon House on London Road and Buxton House on Terrace Road. The natural mineral water baths would always have the edge on these hydros, of course, but it was necessary for the Estate to invest in the most up to date treatments as the medical specialists no doubt demanded.

In the years 1886 to 1888 the Buxton Estate extended the baths in each wing and provided new types of bath including needle, massage and vapour. In 1891 the Hot Baths consisted of 14 Private Baths for ladies and 10 for men and offered needle, Russian, vapour, massage and sitz treatments. The Natural Baths now had five Private Baths each for ladies and gentlemen as well as the Public Baths as before.

New Pump Rooms

In 1882, the St Anne's Well Room, situated in the Natural Baths, had become crowded. In particular there were complaints of charity patients congregating in the colonnade near the well, to the annoyance of visitors. This problem was resolved when the architect Robert R Duke suggested that a Well Room for charity patients be built on George Street, adjoining the new Charity Hot Baths. This was agreed by the charity trustees and the well was built and remains today, still with the inscription 'Devonshire Hospital Drinking Well AD 1882'. The building now houses a large Victorian pump which supplies the mineral water baths at the Devonshire Royal Hospital[29].

As the years went on the St Anne's Well again became crowded and the idea of building a new Well or Pump Room was discussed. Various suggestions were made, including enlargement of the current facility, but in the end a design for a new Pump Room, to be sited at the bottom of the slopes, was accepted. The architect was Henry Currey (this was the last substantial work he did in Buxton before his death in 1900) and the Pump Room was opened in 1894. The Pump Room provided elegant seating

The Crescent showing the Pump Room in the early stages of construction. The scaffolding can be seen to the right of the picture

The Pump Room

arrangements for those wishing to drink either the natural tepid mineral or the chalybeate water. The town guide book of 1905 described the arrangements as:

> '...a polished counter, with a top of veined Italian marble, upon which are
> fixed five massive silvered fountains of suitable design and, through them the
> water flows continuously...whilst the well is open to visitors...'[30]

New provision for free access to the waters was made when the outdoor public double pump of 1855 was replaced in 1894 by a new pump which issued only the natural thermal water. It was sited close to the new Pump Room,

Approaching the 20th Century

By 1896, in addition to the new Pump Room, the accommodation at the Baths had increased. At the Natural Baths were still the two Public Baths for gentlemen and in addition, six Private Baths. The Ladies' provision remained unchanged, with one Public and five Private Baths. In the Hot Baths department there were 22 Private Baths in total, two less than in 1891[31]. It is possible that there had been a reduction in the Gentlemen's side to make way for new forms of bath treatment. At the turn of the century the range of treatments were described as follows:

> '...The Natural Baths, which have a stronger medicinal efficacy, are used only for the
> application of the waters at the natural temperature of the spring [82°F]. They consist of
> separate suites of baths for ladies and gentlemen, and each suite contains both private
> immersion and swimming baths. ...the swimming baths are supplied with a crane and lowering
> chair, and the baths are supplied with the usual douches. The Hot Baths, in which any quantity
> of the natural water, carefully heated, is added to the naturally tepid water, in order to secure
> baths of any temperature that the circumstances of different cases may indicate. The Hot Baths
> have a lower degree of medicinal efficacy, estimated in the proportion of two-thirds - ie. three
> hot baths are estimated to be equal to two natural baths. The immersion baths are lined with
> marble and are entered by a short flight of steps with a protective rail. The water enters from
> apertures in the bottom and a half, three quarter or full bath can be given.
>   The Needle Bath consists of circular metal tubes; each hoop of the tubing is perforated with
> numerous small holes, and when the pressure of water is turned on, emits a small jet or needle
> upon the bather. Combined with this are the ascending and descending wave douches. The
> Buxton Massage and Douche Bath is a flat dish of copper, coated with white metal, in which the
> patient reclines while treatment by douche and massage is applied. Vapour Baths - from
> evaporation of the natural water - may be used either as full bath, in which the patient is encased
> in a wooden box, with a round hole for the head in its movable lid; or in half bath, in which the
> patient is encased to the loins; or local bath, in which any joint may be treated with steam
> derived from the thermal water...'[30]

The main types of disease for which water treatment was being offered were gout, rheumatism, osteo and rheumatoid arthritis, some nervous diseases such as neuralgia, sciatica, tropical diseases such as malarial conditions, heart disease associated with gout or rheumatism, digestive disorders, skin diseases such as gouty eczema, anaemia and phthisis (pulmonary tuberculosis).

Though the use of water treatment is limited today to some forms of physiotherapy, in the nineteenth century it formed a most important branch of medicine. Many different treatments and ways of using the water were developed and many different illnesses were treated, though it must be said that the medical practitioners lacked the diagnostic skills of today's doctors. Nevertheless, Buxton would have considered itself at the forefront of specialist water treatments by the end of the nineteenth century, and many of the resident doctors wrote books on the subject. Dr Robertson's Guide to the use of the Buxton Mineral Waters ran to more than 27 editions and was still being reprinted after his death in 1897.

As we shall see in the next chapter, Buxton continued to develop its water treatments, including the use of electricity in baths.

References
1. White J. Jun, Plan for Improvements at Buxton; 1803 revised 1806. Map 2042, Devonshire Collections, Chatsworth
2. Denman Jos. MD. Op. Cit. 1793 and 1801
3. Buxton Estate Accounts 1806 - 1820, Devonshire Collections, Chatsworth
4. Heacock P. letter 1st January 1810 and earlier correspondence, Letterbooks of P. Heacock, Devonshire Collections, Chatsworth
5. Jewitt A. Op. Cit. 1811
6. Scudamore, Sir Charles MD, A Chemical and Medical Report of the Properties of the Mineral Waters of Buxton, Matlock, Cheltenham [et al] London, 1820 and The Analysis and Medical Properties of the Tepid Springs of Buxton, 3rd edn. London 1839
7. Carstairs, Thomas MD, Bathing and Buxton Waters editions of 1847 and 1853
8. Old Plan of Baths Approaches and the Square as existing prior to the alterations about 1851 Buxton Museum Collection
9. Plan of baths water management, c. 1820, High Peak Borough Council, Buxton.
10. Adam W. Gem of the Peak, editions of 1845 and 1851
11. Buxton Estate Accounts 1820 - 1838, Devonshire Collections, Chatsworth; see also Scudamore, Sir Charles, The Analysis and Medical Account of the Tepid Springs of Buxton 2nd Ed. 1833
12. Orme, Daniel The New Buxton Guide,1823 and The Buxton Guide, 1842

13. Robertson, W.H. Buxton and its Waters, 1838
14. Page T.J. The Buxton Bather's Handbook, Brief Observations on the Buxton Waters, 1843
15. Langham M.J. & Wells C. The Architect of Victorian Buxton, Derbyshire County Library Service, 1996
16. Orme, Daniel The Buxton Guide, 1842 and Pigot & Co.'s Directory of Derbyshire 1835
17. Freebody's Directory of Towns of Derbyshire 1852
18. Auctioneer's catalogue 7.11.1860, Langham & Wells Collection, Buxton
19. Buxton Estate Accounts 1861 - 1891, Devonshire Collections, Chatsworth
20. Croston J. On Foot Through the Peak, 9th edition 1889; Ward Lock, Illustrated Guides to Buxton and the Peak District etc. 1891, 1894; Robinson W.H. Popular Guide to Buxton etc.1896; Baddeley M.J.B. The Peak District of Derbyshire, editions of 1891, 1894
21. Axon E. Op. Cit. paper XVII, 1943
22. Bowden, Annie The Making of the Devonshire Royal Hospital, Buxton, Salford School of Occupational Therapy, unpublished thesis 1991.
23. Builder Magazine, August 20. 1853
24. Chadwick G. F. The Works of Sir Joseph Paxton, 1961, Architectural Press
25. Illustrated London News, August 26. 1854
26. Robertson W.H. A Handbook to the Peak of Derbyshire and to the use of the Buxton Mineral Waters, Buxton 1854
27. Pearson, J. A. Reports of Cases Treated at the Buxton Bath Charity and Devonshire Hospital between May 1st and October 31st 1860, Liverpool 1861
28. Robertson W.H. Op. Cit. Editions of 1861, 1864, 1866, 1868, 1872, 1886
29. Langham M.J. & Wells C. Buxton Waters, Wye Valley Press 1986
30. Buxton Its climate, Baths and Waters, Buxton Medical Society, nd. and Buxton its History, Waters, Climate, Scenery etc. 1905
31. Robertson W.H. A Guide to the use of the Buxton Waters, Buxton, 1896

The Hot Baths after the 1900 remodelling

The Hot Baths after the 1909 addition of glass colonnading

Chapter Four

Changes at the Hot Baths

In 1900 the Hot Baths were remodelled both internally and externally. The shops which had faced the baths from 1863 were demolished and new shop accommodation was made available at the east side of the baths building, by this time known simply as the Colonnade. In place of the old shops were built new waiting and cooling rooms on either side of a central entrance hall from where the bath tickets were issued. The largest addition during this conversion was to the massage department which was housed on the first floor and could be reached by a staircase designed with a very easy gradient for those with walking difficulties. Others too infirm to use the stairs could take advantage of the newly installed hydraulic lift which was situated at the extreme end of the main corridor

Externally the iron and glass colonnading of 1854 was removed and a new classical stone frontage was erected made of tooled ashlar stone taken from the nearby Nithen quarry. The architect for the new frontage was W R Bryden of Buxton and the contractors for the whole of the work were J Parnell & Son of Rugby. Parnell later worked in Buxton on the building of the Empire hotel in 1901-03. The newly converted baths were opened in June 1901[1].

The new stone frontage remained exposed to the elements until 1909, when glass and iron colonnading was erected using much of the old 1854 steelwork and incorporating coloured glass. The architects for the colonnade replacement were Bryden & Walton and the contractors, Messrs G J Bagshaw & Son. The Urban District Council took out a loan of £776 to pay for the replacement of the verandah[2], though a total project cost of only £622 was reported in the Buxton Advertiser.

Bathchairmen

During the early 1900s the bathchair was a common sight in the town, parked in ranks at the bottom of the Slopes in front of the Hot Baths. Other bathchair stands were opposite the Old Hall Hotel, the Broad Walk end of Burlington road and on St John's Road near the church. Bathchairs had been in use in Buxton since the early part of the 19th century, when the town only had one such chair, which was kept at the rear of the Hall Hotel. The three-wheeled chairs were used to convey invalid patients to and from the baths and to various places throughout the town. The chairs protected the passengers from the elements, with a folding front to cover the legs and a folding hood for total comfort. The bathchairman had no such luxuries and hauled his charge around the town, to and from the baths and, not infrequently, to the Cat & Fiddle Inn and the Goyt Valley[3].

Ticket office at the Hot Baths, early 20th century

Entrance to the Hot Baths, early 20th century

Dispensing Well in St Anne's after 1912

The baths become public property

The question of the public purchase of the baths from the Duke of Devonshire was first raised in April 1903 and by January of 1904 it had been agreed for the council to purchase the baths for £25,000, plus an additional annual rent of £1000. The plan was beset by legal difficulties and it became necessary to promote a bill in Parliament. An objection was raised during the passage of the bill through the House of Lords on the grounds that their lordships could not agree to a perpetual annual chief rent. The idea of a chief rent was abandoned and the Natural and Hot Baths were eventually purchased for the sum of £55,000, the council taking out a loan for that amount. The loan was repayable over a period of 60 years with annual payments of £2431, making the total cost of the conveyance, including interest, £145,860.[2/4]

Work at the Pump Room

In 1910 Buxton Corporation appointed Frank Langley as Borough Surveyor and instructed him to submit a report on the general condition of the Natural Baths, which had become somewhat neglected. The findings of this report resulted in a series of excavations at the baths which uncovered a new and abundant source of spring water in front of the Natural Baths. This was at such a level as to allow the nearby pump room to be supplied with gravity fed water from this source, thus removing the need for pumping apparatus to discharge water at the serving counter.

In 1912 work took place to the plans of Langley for major structural changes at the Pump Room. In order to increase the internal floor area the open arcading on the front of the building which had existed since its construction in 1893/4 was enclosed. A well chamber was built at the rear, which contained a sunken marble basin into which the mineral water flowed through holes in its base. The main contractors for the work were largely local people. Robinson Bros of Buxton supplied masons and bricklayers, Edward Brown supplied the joinery, J. Brocklehurst carried out the plastering and the new plumbing was installed by E Broomhead. Much new marble was introduced during this conversion, which was supplied and fitted by the Manchester firm of J & H Patteson. The enlarged Pump Room was reopened to the public on 1st July 1912, by the Duke of Devonshire. After the conversions it was felt that it was no longer strictly accurate to call the building a pump room and it was therefore renamed St Anne's Well. On completion the building had two entrances, one at each end. This soon became a source of irritation to the borough council, since they now had to pay the wages of two, instead of one, ticket attendant. An entrance charge was made at the well which included as many glasses of water as the customer desired. The cost of the conversions was in the region of £2,875 since the UDC took out a loan for that amount, specifically for the reconstruction of St Anne's Well[5].

The converted pump room was very elegant, decorated internally with oak

The Thermal Mineral Baths
= B U X T O N =
(Founded by the Romans)

Recently extended at great cost and now the Most Complete in the Kingdom, embracing one hundred different Medical Treatments:—

Thermal Immersion Baths; Aërated Baths; Buxton Douche Massage; Aix Douche; Vichy Massage sous l'eau; Bourbon-Lancy Treatment; Scotch Douche; Vapour Douche; Needle Douche; Buxton Combination Douche with shower; Needle, Wave, Ascending, Descending or Spinal Douche; Sitz Baths; Plombières Douche; Tivoli Douche; Throat Sprays; Nasal Douches; Eye Irrigations; Fango Mud Baths and Packs; Moor or Peat Baths; Carbonic Acid Gas Baths; Chalybeate Baths; Schwalbach Baths; Nauheim Baths, and Oxygen Baths; Schott Exercises; Electro-Vibratory Massage; d'Arsonval High Frequency Currents; Static Currents; Electric Mineral Water Baths; Schnee Baths; Dowsing Radiant Heat and Light Baths; Cataphoresis, Ionisation, Inunction, Facial Sprays and Massage; Greville Hot-air Baths; Luminous Heat Baths; Thermal Plunge Baths; Full and Local Vapour Baths; Pine, Brine and Sulphur Baths, aerated or still; Bergonie, Dry Massage, Electric Massage, Manicure, Pedicure, etc., etc.

The Most Pleasant Cure for

Rheumatism, Gout, Sciatica, Arthritis, Colitis, Neuritis, Anæmia and Disorders of the Digestion; considerable reputation for the after-treatment of Malaria and other tropical diseases.

Waters Richest in Radio-Activity and <u>Tasteless.</u> Natural temp. 82°F

— ALSO —

CHALYBEATE SPRINGS, rich in proto-carbonate of iron.

ILLUSTRATED HANDBOOK and other literature giving full particulars of Baths and Treatment, Hotels, Hydros and Boarding-houses, from

J. M. SCOTT, Director of Baths, Buxton.

Advertisement of 1909 showing the range of treatments on offer at the Buxton Baths

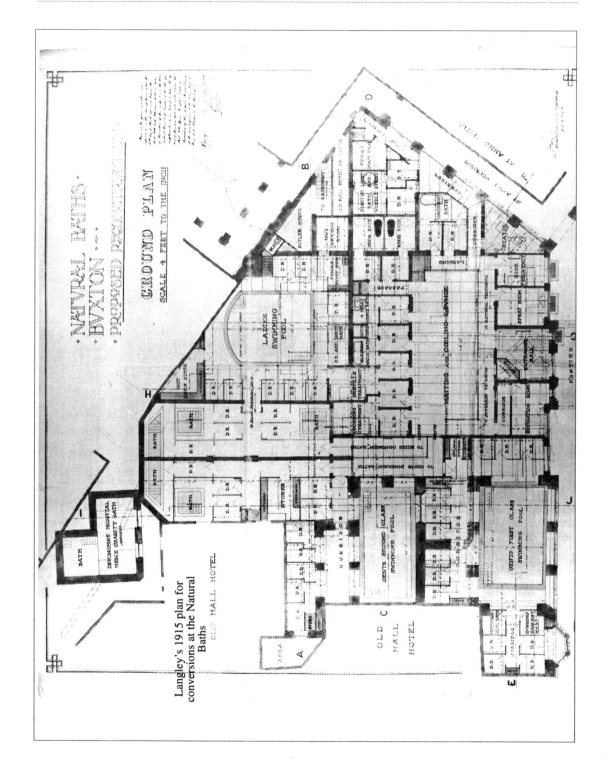

Langley's 1915 plan for conversions at the Natural Baths

Interior of St Anne's Well after 1912 conversion

panelled walls and stained glass windows which still remain today. Two female assistants were employed at the marble pool, one ladling the water from the pool with a glass in a holder on the end of a long metal pole. The other assistant took the glass from the holder and passed the full glass to the customer who waited at the other side of the marble balustrading surrounding the pool.

Treatments at the baths

By 1909 the Buxton baths were advertising many and varied treatments. At the Natural Baths there remained separate swimming baths for ladies and gentlemen. Doctors Armstrong & Harburn, who were practising in Buxton in 1911, recommended an immersion in the swimming baths of between 5 and 12 minutes and patients were encouraged to move their limbs as much as possible whilst in the bath to liberate the gases contained in the water. The douche was often used in conjunction with a visit to the bath and a recommended bath of 8 minutes duration would consist of a 4 minute swim, a 2 minute douche followed by a further 2 minute swim[6].

In addition to the Buxton Douche Massage, the vapour baths and the needle baths mentioned in the previous chapter, the Hot Baths offered a multitude of ways to apply water to the body. Sitz baths were available, which were shallow baths, big enough for only one person to immerse trunk and thighs. The Plombiere Douche (spa water enema, first introduced in the French town of Plombiere) was much in demand. Also on offer were the Aix and Vichy douches (similar to the Buxton douche massage). In the Aix douche the patient sat upright in a chair as 1 or 2 attendants performed massage whilst running streams of hot water over the body. The Vichy massage was different in that the patient reclined in a bath on a hot water mattress and massage was applied with the hot water flowing over the body[7].

More baths conversions

Although it was intended to modernise and extend the Natural Baths in 1912, financial and other considerations caused the council to concentrate their efforts on improvements at the Hot Baths. At the time more treatments were dispensed and the greatest revenue came from the Hot Baths. Frank Langley designed a series of changes which seem to have been largely decorative, involving extensive use of wall tiling and the installation of much marble. The modernisation work was completed in time for the 1913 season at a cost of £6000.

The plans for a major upgrading at the Natural Baths, which had been prepared by Langley, had been subjected to much delay but were finally approved in 1914. The intervention of World War I further delayed the implementation of the scheme. During the following years a number of amended plans were submitted to the council for consideration and it was not until 1922, following a loan of £19,500 from the Ministry of Health, that work on the conversions began. We have been able to identify two plans which relate to this work, one dating to April 1915, the other to December 1921[8]. Using these plans for guidance we can see that new types of baths and new plunge baths were built during this reconstruction, together with rooms to house the new electrical treatments within the building. The room housing the Gentlemen's first class bath was extended and the floor of the bath was paved with Sicilian marble slabs which were perforated to allow the gas which is naturally released from the spring to rise through the water.

The three large swimming pools (Gents 1st class, Gents 2nd class and Ladies) were renovated but remained largely unchanged from their layout in 1853. Adjacent to the Gentlemen's Second Class Bath a new connection was made to the first floor of the Old Hall Hotel, thus providing a covered passage from the hotel to the baths. The south facade of the baths was completely remodelled in the same style and materials as used by Currey in 1853. The facade was raised, the balustrading altered and the stonework in the piers redesigned. Changes were made to the ticket office and entrance hall and the work also included the modelling of the present entrance to the baths from the road side using Darley Dale Ashlar stone. The floors of the public rooms were paved in black and white marble and the walls were lined with Carrara Arni Vein marble and Kerry red marble bands. The whole building was re-roofed, replacing the earlier ridge and furrow roof. The main contractor for the work was J Ridyard & Son of Ashton under Lyne. The newly reconstructed baths were opened in May 1924 by the President of the Royal College of Physicians, Sir Humphrey Rolleston[9]. In addition to the three

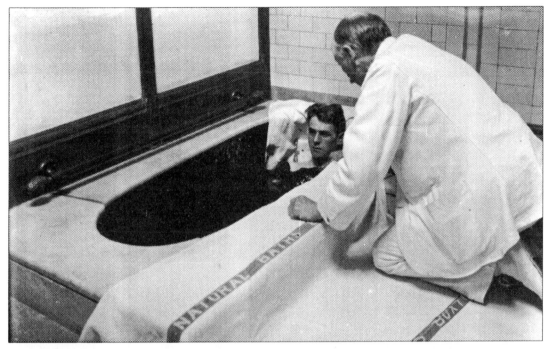

Patient receiving a Peat Bath

Patient receiving water douche after peat treatment

Gentlemen's first class bath, Natural Bath

Ladies' first class bath, Natural Bath

large pools there were now three Ladies and three Gents private immersion baths. A number of small new rooms were set aside for the exclusive dispensing of one particular treatment, including the Electric Water bath, three Moor baths, a Nauheim bath, Static and High Frequency rooms and two Greville treatment rooms. The Greville treatment involved the blowing of super heated air on to the affected part of the body prior to immersion in a warm bath. The Greville equipment had been purchased in 1920 using a loan of £700. The use of electricity in conjunction with the water treatment had gradually become more popular and by the 1920s had reached its peak. The combination of water and electrical current may sound rather frightening but many variants of such treatments were on offer at the Natural Baths. There were the Electro-water bath, the four-cell Schnee bath, the D'Arsonval High Frequency and the Dowsing Radiant Light & Heat Treatment. Popular, perhaps for its novelty value, was the Electric Light Bath which consisted of a wardrobe like arrangement which was fitted with electric light bulbs on its inner surfaces. The patient stood in the middle of this chamber and in some cases was sprayed with a water douche.

Electro-vibratory massage was available and Fango mud treatments were given, using mud specially imported from Fango, Italy. A room at the front of the Natural Baths building housed the Nauheim Bath, which used effervescent salt water as introduced from the German spa of Bad Nauheim. Guide books of 1924 feature a new addition to the treatment list, the Whirlpool Bath, which was specially adapted for limbs affected by gunshot wounds, cases of which would not have been scarce given the recent 1914-18 war.

The Natural Baths offered the popular Peat or Moor baths, which were housed in three bathing cubicles. Each cubicle housed a small bath and a bath shaped hole in a raised slab of marble. The hole looked down into the baths basement where specially constructed peat trucks ran on two foot gauge rails. When filled with their peat mixture, the trucks were trundled into position under the hole in the marble slab and a sliding door was closed behind it. The naked patient lowered himself into the truck and lay immersed up to the neck for about twenty minutes. A careful eye was kept on the peat bather by the bath attendant because some could not take the whole treatment and needed to be extracted from the bath early. The patient was then hosed down with a fine needle spray in the small bath and wrapped in hot towels for a further twenty minutes. When the patient finally vacated the cubicle the bath attendant rang a bell and the boilerman wheeled back the truck into the cellar and disposed of the used peat through an earthenware pipe which drained into a culvert leading to the river Wye.

The moor baths were prepared by the boilerman which took some time and it was thus necessary to make an appointment for such baths. He put a quantity of peat into the truck and added water which was stirred using a paddle. Steam was then introduced into the mixture, raising the temperature to anything from 90°F to 105°F (32-40°C). The

Remains of a peat truck under the Natural Bath

water used in the peat mixture was originally taken from the chalybeate source in the belief that its high iron content mixed with the acidic peat enhanced the efficacy of the treatment. By 1953 the iron pipes which were used to carry the chalybeate water had become badly corroded, compromising the pureness of supply, and mineral or ordinary tap water was used instead. The trucks and rails remain under the baths and are still in remarkably good condition. Peat for these baths was taken from the moors on the southern side of the Cat & Fiddle road and was stored in a building at Burbage reservoir until needed, when it was brought by lorry to the rear of the baths and tipped into the cellar[16].

The Charity baths change premises

As we have seen in the previous chapter, Buxton's foremost water physician, Dr WH Robertson, had argued strenuously that the water would lose its healing properties if it was moved too far from its source. This resulted in the compromise solution to site the Charity Baths of 1876 in George Street and behind the Old Hall Hotel. Robertson died in 1897 and his successors probably did not hold such strong beliefs, because in 1914 new Charity Baths were provided in a purpose built unit on ground adjoining the south of the Devonshire Hospital building. These new baths were obviously more convenient for the infirm patients at the hospital and could be reached by a walkway from the interior of the dome. The old Charity Hot and Natural Baths were closed, but the water for the new baths was pumped from the Bath Charity Drinking Well building of 1882 in George Street, using a gravity pump which still exists within the building today[10].

The Buxton Clinic

Affluent health seekers continued to be treated at the Hot and Natural Baths and the poor continued to receive treatment at the Devonshire Hospital through the Bath Charity. It seems, however, that by the 1930s it was felt that there was a niche in the market to provide bathing facilities for the *'middle class patient with limited means'*. This led to the formation of a company known as the Buxton Clinic Ltd, under the chairmanship of Mr W. F. Wrigley. The Buxton Clinic was situated in the east wing of the Crescent and was officially opened by Lord Horder (physician to the Prince of Wales) on April 26th 1935. Patients from the clinic received their treatment at the adjacent Hot Baths and had the use of lounges, writing rooms, billiards and a library. Social functions were held at the clinic and the patients' dining room was housed in the assembly room on the first floor of the building. Residents were also granted free entry into the Pavilion Gardens during their period of treatment.

In 1935 the Clinic was advertising accommodation for 110 patients '... *At a cost within the means of the middle classes...*'[11]. The price of one week's treatment at the clinic ranged from 4 to 6 guineas (£4.20 - £6.30) and the recommended period of treatment was three weeks. In April 1938 the Clinic completed a scheme of extension, adding two floors to the establishment

Beginnings of Decline in Water Treatment

The Buxton Corporation Accounts of December 1937 show that the baths and wells undertaking was £1000 down on the previous year. Working expenditure on both sets of baths rose from £6838 to £7534 but income from treatments fell from £6139 to £5800 and after the addition of £102 miscellaneous income the net trading deficiency was £1452[2]. It is interesting to compare this loss with the healthy trading figures at the baths during the height of their popularity, as recorded in chapter 3, where we have seen, for example, the Natural & Hot Baths taking an average annual net profit of £4000 in the 1870s, peaking in 1878 with a net profit of £5000. Despite the falling income from the baths a visit from the British Health Resorts Association in 1938 resulted in a very satisfactory report on Buxton's bathing facilities.

After the Second World War (1939-1945) increasing public apathy to the water cure continued. Comparison of the Langley 1924 changes and plans of about 1950 suggest that there must have been at least one major redesign of the Natural Baths interior between these dates. The later plans graphically illustrate the declining popularity of the electrical treatments which had been so sought after in the early part of the century. Gone were the Greville rooms, the Electric Light Baths, the Dowsing Radiant Heat rooms, the 4 cell Schnee Baths, the Spray room and the emanation room[13]. The introduction of the National Health Service in 1948 did not help the fortunes of the baths. It had been hoped that the new NHS would take over spa establishments throughout the country, thus giving the Buxton baths a sound financial footing. In the event spas were excluded from the NHS, but the Borough Council won a minor concession from the government. This allowed for spa treatment to be financed by the NHS at the Devonshire Royal Hospital, if such treatment was prescribed by a doctor. Following the introduction of the NHS the Buxton Clinic was annexed to the Devonshire Royal Hospital and spa water treatments could be obtained under the Health Service until 1963[16].

The Natural Baths

Whilst traditional bathing medicine declined at the Natural Baths, a range of physiotherapy treatments were developed. A guide book of 1946 showed three pools in use for remedial exercises and swimming under trained supervision. Also on offer were aeration, immersion and peat baths, and ultra violet and paraffin wax treatments. Guide books of 1950 show that the Hubbard Tank, artificial sunlight and diathermy were available and plans of about the same time show an extra Moor bath which fits in with the generally held opinion that the Peat or Moor bath had a lingering popularity and was one of the last of the treatments to be phased out.

Hot Baths interior c1935

Gentlemens' corridor, Hot Baths, 1935

Ladies' corridor, Hot Baths, 1935

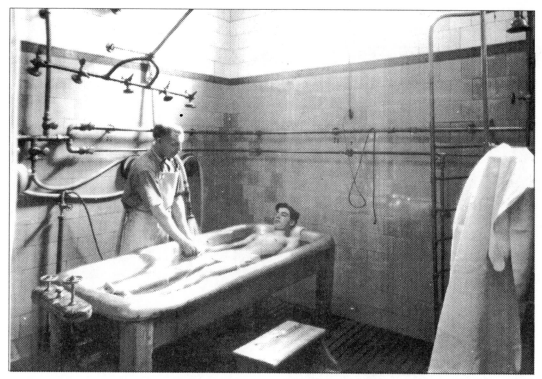

Buxton massage and douche bath

The Hot Baths

As we know, the Hot Baths used the natural mineral water which was heated to various temperatures depending on the nature of the treatment. The natural water was piped from the Natural Baths, across the front of the Crescent into a long tank under the road in front of the Hot Baths facade. From there it was piped to two tanks at the rear of the building and then to two further tanks in the water tower in the centre of the building. There were two boilers housed in the baths, which were in constant use during the day and the boilerman was kept busy attending the boilers and mixing peat for baths and packs. The boilerman started his day at 7am, so that the water could be heated in time for the arrival of the patients, and he also worked in the evenings and on Sundays, after the baths were closed, to stoke the boilers. One of the two boilers was a Cornish type with a vertical boiler and the other was a Lancashire boiler which had two horizontal barrels. The coke to power the boilers came from the Buxton Gasworks until 1962, when these gasworks closed and coke was then brought from Chesterfield. A large amount of linen was used at the baths in the shape of towels, peat sheets, uniforms and a laundry was on site to deal with it. This laundry was housed in the Hot Baths complex but dealt with the washing from the Natural Baths and St Anne's Well (the former Pump Room) as well as its own. Hannah Nall was the sole washerwoman and she was

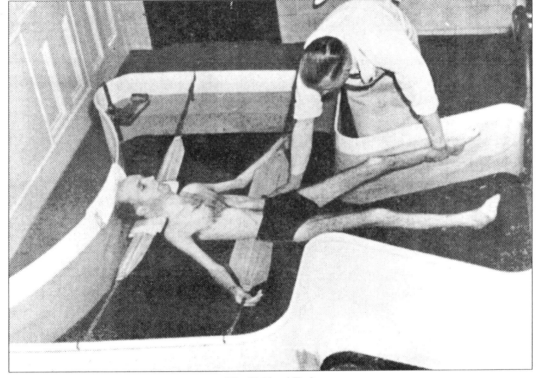

The Hubbard Tank

equipped with an industrial washing machine.

After the Charity Hot Baths in George Street became redundant in 1914, part of the building was used as public wash baths, which were frequented by the town's residents whose houses did not have bathrooms of their own. The hot water for the baths was provided by the boilerman at the Hot Baths and a bath, in the 1940s, cost 6d (2p). In 1947 four new public wash baths were built beside the Hot Baths boilerhouse[16].

The Hot Baths in the 1950s
In the 1950s the Hot Baths could still offer a large range of treatments and the complex contained 13 immersion pools for ladies and 6 for gentlemen, 3 vapour baths for ladies and 4 for gentlemen, together with separate rooms for treatments such as: the Plombiere Douche, the Aix Douche, Buxton Douche Massage, peat packs, liver packs and various heat treatments. Each treatment was separately priced and inclusive tickets for two or three weeks of treatment could be bought. Plans dating to 22nd January 1952 suggest that alteration and reconstruction of the roof of the ladies' Douche Massage Department on the first floor of the Hot Baths may have been carried out at that time or was certainly contemplated[12].

In the 1950s football teams were regular visitors to the Hot Baths. As well as the two Manchester teams, Nottingham Forest, Notts County, both Sheffield teams, Newcastle United, Blackpool, Leicester City, Cardiff City, Everton, Middlesborough and Southampton all came. Typically, they would stay at the Palace Hotel for a couple of days and take tonic aeration baths and Buxton Douche Baths to tone them up for their matches. Some players had injuries which were helped by Buxton treatment[16].

Alternative Uses for the Natural Baths

Treatments at the Natural Baths finished in 1954 and all the treatments and treatment staff were moved to the Hot Baths. This left the three large pools in the building available for swimmers and thus it became the town's public swimming baths. Many of the town's residents will remember these baths, particularly the Gentlemen's first class bath which was built over the main thermal spring and was floored with perforated slabs which allowed the water and bubbles of gas to enter the pool. The water, when seen in quantity in a pool of that size, showed its natural pale blue colouring which is not seen in many other waters. The second of the pools, the Gentlemen's second class bath, was less popular with swimmers because of its lack of natural lighting, but the Ladies' bath, with its bright lighting from the glass roof was pleasant, if small. Even though the baths were given over to the use of swimmers it was still believed that immersion in the thermal water should be subject to a time limit, as the waters were apt

Hot Baths during conversion in 1985

to induce tiredness. When the bather handed in their clothes for safe keeping, draped on a metal frame designed for the purpose, a note was taken of the number and time of entering the bath. After the allotted time the attendant called out the number at the poolside and the bather was obliged to get out and get dressed. After 1961 the time allowed was increased to 30 minutes[16].

As the popularity of the baths continued to diminish, new uses were found for the facilities. In the 1950s the oak panelled cooling room was hired out to various private organisations including the Old Peoples' Welfare Coordinating Committee, the Professional Womens' Club, the Gospel Hall and the Fencing Club in order to raise income. The minutes of the Baths and Wells Committee of 1950 record an agreement to give the exclusive use of the Gentlemen's second class pool to the Divisional Education Committee to provide swimming instruction for school children. In June 1959 the Gentlemen's first class bath was hired by Jehovah's Witnesses for the purpose of a mass baptism[10].

Closure of the Hot Baths

Despite the range of treatments on offer at the Hot Baths, patient numbers declined from the mid 1950s and representations were made to the Regional Hospital Board expressing concern over the decreasing use of the Hot Baths by the NHS. In 1962 the Lancashire boiler developed a serious fault and was condemned, leaving only the Cornish boiler. When this boiler had to be descaled a few months later no wet treatments were performed for a period of eight days[16].

In 1963 a new deep hydrotherapy pool was installed in the Devonshire Hospital thus obviating, at a stroke, the need for the hospital patients to visit the baths. This is borne out by a report in June 1963 from the Baths' manager to the Bath and Wells Committee stating that there had been a sudden drop in the number of treatments given at the baths, from 454 patients in one week to only 102 the following week. Despite the immediate dismissal of 3 hydrotherapy assistants, one receptionist, a boilerman and a cleaner, the Hot baths were obviously no longer viable and closed on 30th September 1963[10]. One of the bath attendants at the Hot Baths, Mary Hargreaves, who had administered Peat, Aeration baths and Buxton Douch Massages for thirty years, said of the closure *'The water is God's gift to the town and it is being thrown away'*[16]. The Buxton Clinic, in the east wing of the Crescent, closed in June 1963.

Closure of the Natural baths

The Natural Baths were closed for three months beginning in May 1957 in order to install new chlorinating apparatus and fit scum channels. In 1959 dry rot was found in the building, and the baths closed on 9 February of that year. Although the closure of the baths was probably intended to be permanent, the public pressure for swimming

St Anne's Well in 1996, still retaining many of its original features.

In 1996 the humidity in the Ladies' Natural Bath supports flora,
perhaps anticipating the new life planned for the baths.

facilities appeared to persuade the council to reopen the the baths on a temporary basis in 1961[16].

Despite this temporary intention the baths remained in use as public swimming baths throughout the 1960s, despite being closed regularly for short periods for essential repairs[10]. A new public swimming bath at the Pavilion Gardens was commenced in 1969 by the architectural practice of J Poulson, but completed by Booth, Hancock & Johnson of Pontefract. It was opened by Princess Anne in November 1972, at which time the Natural Baths were closed. Over time the Natural Baths building remained empty and concern was expressed about its likely rapid deterioration. However, English Heritage, together with the High Peak Borough Council, have ensured that the baths are kept wind and weather tight.

It is ironic that the town should have invested in a 60 year mortgage to buy the baths in 1904 only to see them close a year prior to the loan being repaid.

New Use for the Hot Baths

The 1909 glass and iron colonnading fronting the Hot Baths was taken down in the 1960s due to its unsafe condition, but the colonnading around the corner, on the east side of the building remained and was restored by the Borough Council in 1975. Similarly the colonnading across the road fronting the Grove Hotel and the west end of Spring Gardens remains, and has been restored in recent years. In 1985/6 the Hot Baths building, which had deteriorated markedly after its closure, was converted into a shopping centre, the Cavendish Arcade, at a cost of £598,000.

The architect for the project was Derek Latham and the contractors were the Chapel en le Frith building company, G D Rogers. Although the baths were removed during this conversion, effort was made to preserve something of the baths' heritage and a small plunge bath (referred to as a Deep Pool on a 1963 plan) has been restored within the complex and the original wall tiling has been retained. Another, smaller bath has been retained and can be seen inside one of the shops under a metal grating. The completed arcade was topped with a 3,000 square feet barrel vaulted, stained glass roof designed by the artist Brian Clarke at an additional cost of £100,000[14].

Further changes at St Anne's Well

The 1894 free outdoor public pump adjacent to St Anne's Well was replaced in 1940 by the present pump. Inscribed '*A well of living waters*', it was dedicated to Emilie Dorothy Bounds, Councillor of the Borough, by her husband and daughter.

At St Anne's Well (the former Pump Room) water could still be taken from the marble pool but by the 1950s only one assistant was employed in an effort to reduce costs. To achieve this, a swan neck pipe was installed above the pool which poured the thermal water into the pool from above, unlike the previous arrangement when the pool

St Anne's Well, present day, showing the curved feed pipe which was installed in the 1950s

had been filled from below. Since the glasses could be filled directly from this pipe only one assistant was required. Water could still be drawn from the dispensing pool at the well in the 1970s, when the building housed the Tourist Information Centre but access to the pool was terminated when the Micrarium took over the premises in the early 1980s. The Micrarium was almost unique in the world, and showed the microscopic world of animal and plant life through a selection of projection microscopes. Due to the retirement of the proprietor the Micrarium has recently closed which, whilst denying the town this unique feature, leaves the building empty and available for renovation, perhaps to something approaching its former use.

The Natural Baths building today houses the Tourist Information Centre, the main part of which is situated in the former oak panelled Cooling Room. Through a window at the centre can still be seen the remains of the Great or Gentlemen's first class bath. It has been greatly reduced in size and is now covered by a perspex dome to prevent contamination. It is from this point, the main spring, that water is taken for bottling purposes and to supply St Anne's public well across the road. Within the same room is housed an underground tank which holds the water prior to being pumped to the town's spa water swimming pool at the Pavilion Gardens and the Devonshire Royal Hospital. The small fountain in front of the Crescent is also fed from this tank and the remaining unused water is diverted into the river Wye, as required by the National Rivers' Authority.

Bottled Buxton Water

Bottled water was sold by the Buxton Corporation in the first part of the century, a guide book of 1927 offered 'Buxton Table Water', sparkling or still, in baby, small, medium and large sizes, suggesting that the larger size was most suitable for those wishing to supplement their treatment at home. By the middle of the century the water was being bottled by the Apollinaris Company from premises on George Street. In June 1955 they terminated their lease and the premises were taken over by Schweppes, and then again in November 1955, by the local firm, Tebbs Mineral Water Company, who not only bottled the spring water but also used the plant for the bottling of soft drinks and beer. Tebbs were taken over by Canada Dry Rawlings in the 1980s and bottling of the water in still and carbonated form continued through their subsidiary of Hooper Struve and Company Ltd, who continued to trade under the name Buxton Water Company. From their premises in the old Hot Charity Baths in George Street the company produced 600,000 bottles annually[10].

The company was again taken over in 1987, this time by Perrier (UK) Ltd who dramatically increased the amount of bottling in an ever increasing market. In 1989 the company moved to a purpose built site near Buxton railway station, which houses one of the most technically advanced bottling plants in Britain. The water is taken from the spring source to the bottling plant in specially laid stainless steel pipes. In addition to the still and carbonated versions the present company offer the water with orange or lemon/lime flavouring in sizes ranging from 50cl to 5 litres. EC regulations now define the term 'Mineral Water' very specifically and Buxton water, which satisfies this definition, is termed 'Buxton Natural Mineral Water'.

Buxton water is now the best selling English Mineral Water and in 1984, 35 million bottles were produced. In 1995 the company invested £3.8 million in a new plant extension which increased production to 90 million bottles a year. The company presently employs sixty people[15].

Epilogue

Today the 'water cure' is no longer available at Buxton and the thermal water, which for so long was the reason for thousands of invalids to travel to the town, is no longer credited with the healing properties of its heyday. A recent resurgence in the consumption of bottled waters throughout the country has given Buxton water a new 'raison d'etre' for the foreseeable future.

Clarendon Hydro

The major refurbishment of the Georgian Crescent, completed in 1996, will hopefully pave the way for work to be done on the Natural Baths and the Pump Room, with the possibility of re-introducng some aspects of the Buxton Spa heritage, but will water bathing treatments at Buxton ever regain the popularity of their boom years? We live in hope!

References
1. Buxton Advertiser editions of: 29 December 1900; 9 March; 11 May; 1 June; 22 June 1901; Buxton Library, Local Studies
2. Buxton Baths Capital Expenditure Accounts, Langham & Wells papers, Buxton
3. Leach John, The Book of Buxton. Barracuda Books. 1987
4. Buxton Advertiser editions of: 24 April 1903; 23 January 1904; 9 April; 21 May; 31 December 1904
5. Buxton Advertiser 30 July 1912
6. Armstrong Wm & Harburn J.E. Buxton, Its waters, baths and accessory methods of treatment. 1911. John Wright & Sons, Bristol
7. Hyde Samuel MD. Buxton, Its Baths and Climate. John Heywood, Deansgate and Ridgefield, Manchester 1895
8. Natural Baths, Buxton, Proposed Reconstruction Ground Plan 1915 and ditto 1921, Engineer & Surveyor, Buxton Borough Council
9. Buxton Advertiser 17 May 1924
10. Langham M J & Wells C . 0p. Cit. 1986
11. Buxton Advertiser April 26th 1935
12. Buxton Thermal Baths 1952-63 3 Plans, Derbyshire Record Office, Matlock.
13. Mineral Water Baths, St Anne's Well, Wash Baths and bottling stores, undated plan, Langham & Wells collection, Buxton
14. Buxton Advertiser editions of 1986
15. Personal correspondence with Buxton Mineral Water Company 1996
16. Bradshaw, Ray, Working Life of Buxton 1947-63, Private Research papers

The following Buxton Guides have also been used in writing this chapter:

- Buxton Guide Book, John Hatton. 1909. Buxton Advertising Committee;
- Buxton The Mountain Spa, 1912 Bureau of Information, Buxton.
- In And Around Buxton. 1920. Edited by J M Scott;
- Bonny Buxton, Derbyshire. 1924. Bureau of Information, Buxton;
- A Guide to Buxton: its Baths, Gardens, etc. Abel Heywood & Sons Ltd. Manchester undated.
- Buxton. The Spa of Blue waters. 1937, 1938, 1940
- Buxton. For entertainment all the year round. 1951, 1952, Borough of Buxton
- Buxton Official Guide. 1955, 1961, Borough of Buxton
- Buxton for Health and Holidays. 1958, Borough of Buxton.
- Buxton The Mountain Spa, Buxton Borough c.1921
- Guidebook of Buxton, 1948. Peak Publications
- Buxton Beautiful & Romantic c.1927. Borough of Buxton.
- Buxton Calling 1925. Borough of Buxton
- Guide to Buxton Ward Lock 1915 & 1948.

Appendix 1

The Buxton baths offered a great variety of water treatments. Many new forms of treatment were developed in the latter part of the 19th century. The advent of electricity to the town in 1900 saw the introduction of electro-water cures which expanded the range still further. Below we give descriptions of the treatments mentioned in the book.

Aeration Bath
Certain of the small immersion baths at the Hot baths were fitted with aeration apparatus consisting of small holes in the bath walls which could be used to pump air into the bath rather like today's jacuzzi. The recommended length of immersion in an aeration bath was 45 minutes and was usually followed by a hot towel wrap of 20 minutes duration. (See whirlpool bath.)

Aix Douche Massage
The patient sat upright in a chair whilst attendants poured streams of hot water over the body and applied massage.

Ascending Douche
A perforated seat arrangement in which water was forced under pressure through perforations vertically to the seated patient. Recommended for haemorrhoids, rectal and uterine prolapses, uterine congestions and painful or irregular menstruation. The treatment could also be effected through a jet or spray from a nozzle placed near the level of the floor, when it could be used on the soles of the feet. Treatment was offered in a range of water temperatures to suit particular medical conditions.

Buxton Douche Massage
The patient received this treatment whilst lying in a shallow bath of copper coated with white metal. The water depth was about 7 or 8 inches at a temperature of 93-98°F (34-36°C) Water was forced onto the body at a temperature of 96-102°F (35-38°C) via a douche hose and massage applied. The treatment lasted 10-15 minutes. Sometimes the douche massage was followed by a douche spray down the spine of the erect patient. The spray was gradually lowered in temperature to as cold as the patient could stand. Following this the patient was wrapped in towels and allowed to rest in the dressing room before dressing.

Buxton Oxygen Bath
It is difficult to identify this treatment for certain, but in the USA there was a treatment called the air bath in which the patient was simply laid on a bed and the assistant either opened the window or directed a fan at the body to circulate the air. It can be assumed with a degree of certainty that if the Buxton Oxygen Bath approximated the American Air Bath, there would be few takers during the winter!

Chalybeate Bath Hot and cold baths using chalybeate or iron-bearing water

Douche
The application of a single or multiple column of water against some part of the body. Various types of hose and nozzles were used and treatments varied in relation to temperature, pressure and mass of water used, according to the type of complaint being treated. The douche was a widely used form of treatment and many variations existed eg. horizontal jet, vertical jet, fan, broken jet. Special applications of the douche to particular parts of the body or internal organs were separately named eg. dorsal, lumbar, cerebral or gastric douches.

Wet Douche	Douche applied when patient is immersed in a bath (sometimes referred to as the undercurrent).
Dry Douche	Applied directly to body of patient, usually erect.
Descending Douche	What we now know as a shower.

Facial Massage   Local massage or 'shampooing' of the face.

Fango Mud Packs
A mud made from dark volcanic ash, imported from Italy, and
mineral water is applied to the affected part of the body. It is
supposed to draw the toxins out of the pores and cure arthritic
pains.

Greville Heat Treatment
Super heated air was applied to the affected part of the
body prior to immersion in a warm bath.

Hand bath

Hubbard tank
Shallow tank in which the patient was laid and
supported by slings in a floating position. Massage
and exercises were given by an attendant.

Hydropathy and Hydrotherapy
General terms appertaining to the treatment of
disease by the use of water internally or externally.
The term Hydriatric or Hydriatic was used in the early part of the 20th century, meaning relating to, or
characteristic of the treatment of diseases by water. From Hydropathy we obtain Hydropathic or Hydro
meaning a hotel or boarding house at a pleasure resort which provides facilities for the treatment of
patients by hydropathy.

Immersion Bath (& local)
General term meaning immersion in a single bath such as that found in an ordinary bathroom. These
baths could be taken as 'full', 'three-quarter' or 'half' baths (the latter two being specially indicated in
cases where there was cardiac weakness). They were administered at varying temperatures. One variant,
called the Graduated Bath commenced at a temperature between 93-98°F (34-36°C) and the temperature
was decreased in successive baths.

Manicure   Cosmetic treatment of the hands & fingernails.

Matlock Bath   Bath given at temperature of 68°F, simulating the waters of the fashionable Matlock spring.

Medicated Bath (Pine, Brine & Sulphur)
A bath prepared with the type of additional medication as described. It is possible to conjecture that such
baths were replicating the kind of treatment found elsewhere, brine for example, at the Nauheim baths
or sulphur the baths at Bath in Somerset.

Moor (or Peat) Bath
Moor peat was mixed with water and heated by steam injection to a temperature of 90-105°F (32-40°C)
to form a paste. The recommended time of immersion in the bath was about twenty minutes, but because
the hot mixture could induce drowsiness some patients bathed for lesser time. After emerging from the
peat the patient was hosed down by the bath assistant and wrapped in hot towels for a further twenty
minutes. The treatment was considered effective for skin disorders, rheumatism & sciatica. The peat bath
induced profuse sweating and often resulted in a temporary loss of weight. The peat was obtained from
the moors surrounding Buxton. A variation of this bath was the peat Sitz bath which immersed the lower
torso and thighs in a small bath filled with the peat mixture.

Page 95
Chalybeate
Bath

Moor Pack
This was designed for those who could not, or preferred not to take the full peat bath. It was designed to treat individual joints. The patient was laid on a slatted wooden plinth which was covered with a rubber sheet topped with a sheet of calico. The hot peat mixture was packed around the affected joint and the sheet was wrapped around the peat. The pack was left in place for twenty minutes, after which it was removed and the joint was either sponged clean or the patient took an immersion bath.

Mustard Bath   As the medicated bath but containing mustard powder

Mustard Pack   Mustard and water mixed to a thick paste and applied to the affected area

Nauheim Bath
Effervescent saline bath found naturally in the resort of Nauheim (Bad Nauheim) in Germany. The water there is heavily charged with carbonic acid gas (carbon dioxide) and contains, in solution, a large amount of calcium chloride. The bath was artificially prepared in Buxton and elsewhere by the addition of several chemicals, including carbonate of soda and hydrochloric acid, in particular proportions, to the natural mineral water. It was felt to be very effective in the cure of cardiac and renal cases

Needle Bath (or Douche en Circle).
A series of nearly circular pipes arranged on top of each other which were perforated on their inner surfaces. water was forced through the pipes under pressure, emitting small jets or needles of water on the patient who stood in the middle of the apparatus. The equipment often incorporated the rain or shower douche and the ascending douche.

Pedicure   Cosmetic treatment of the feet and toenails.

Plombiere Douche   Mineral water enema. First introduced in the French town of Plombiere. Used in cases of colonic disorders.

Russian Bath
In this bath the patient lay on a slab in a small room filled with steam. The temperature would range from 115 to 120 °F (46 to 48°C) and the length of the bath 10 to 20 minutes. The treatment might include alternate heat and cold with the patient moving between the steam room and a cold shower. In a Russian Bath the patient would be rubbed by an attendant to promote the early appearance of perspiration. Ailments treated by this method include rheumatic pain, diabetes, dyspepsia and sciatica

Sand Bath
Sand was heated to the temperature of 110-120° F (43-48°C) on iron plates. The sand was mixed to obtain an even temperature and applied to the extremities of the patient in a layer 3-4 inches thick and to the abdomen and chest half an inch thick. This encouraged profuse perspiration and formed a crust of sand over the skin which was afterwards washed off by a warm bath. Considered effective in cases of gout, rheumatism and Bright's Disease

Scottish Douche
Two hoses were used alternately, one hot the other cold which were sprayed under pressure to the standing patient. The hot application was relatively long (1-4 minutes) whilst the cold was short (3-30 seconds). The application could be applied to a large area of the body or more localised. It was considered good for cases of paralysis, neurasthenia, sciatica and gout.

Shampooing   Would be referred to nowadays as massaging

Sitz Bath   Small portable bath, made of metal, porcelain or wood of such a form and size that the patient could be seated in it by leaving the feet outside the bath. The lower trunk and upper thighs only were immersed in the Sitz bath and could be taken hot or cold and with or without a douche. Used for conditions of the lower spine, and genitalia.

Sprays   A form of Douche where, instead of a single jet, the water issues from a perforated head in a considerable number of small streams. Fine water sprays were applied to the throat, nose, ears & eyes.

Sun Bath   In the American version of this treatment the patient was undressed and laid out in front of a south facing window to bathe in the sun's rays for about 15 minutes. The Buxton version of this may approximate to the Oxygen Bath, certainly the salubrity of the air in Buxton was much advertised in the 19th and early 20th centuries.

Terrain Cure

Buxton was noted for this, so called 'Terrain Cure' or graduated hill climbing. The exercise was thought to be a valuable part of the treatment for heart weakness and early forms of cardiac degeneration. The terrace slopes in front of the baths at Buxton was considered ideal for this purpose, both doctor and patient could measure the improvement as the patient climbed progressively higher.

Turkish Bath

An early form of bath dating, at least to Roman times. The Turkish Bath suite in the early 20th century would consist of: a warm room (tepidarium), a hot room (calidarium), a douche apparatus, a plunge bath, shampoo room and a cooling room. Dry heat was used in these rooms, which were usually communal and various forms of exercise or massage would accompany the stay in each room. In this description the term 'shampoo' means washing the patient with soap and water and a rough cloth mitten. The usual routine was the warm room followed by the hot room, shampooing, douche and then the plunge bath.

Vapour Bath

Essentially a steam bath. In some cases the patient was enclosed in a cabinet with only the head protruding. Alternatively the half vapour bath enclosed the lower trunk and lower limbs only. Local versions of the apparatus were available to treat individual limbs.

Vichy douche

Similar to the Buxton Douche Massage, the patient reclining in a shallow bath, lying on a hot water mattress. Water was applied to the body and massage given.

Wax Treatments

Introduced into Buxton in 1946, the wax treatment was designed to give relief to patients with rheumatic conditions of the hands and wrists. The affected hand was immersed in a small bath of melted wax for a few seconds. This process was repeated several times, with the patient keeping the fingers perfectly still so as to avoid cracking of the wax.

Whirlpool Bath

Small bath for one person with swirling and bubbling water. Equivalent to today's Jacuzzi.

Electrical Treatments

Artificial Sunlight
Exposure of the body to ultraviolet rays, equivalent to present day solariums.

Bergonie Chair
We are unable to discover what was involved in this treatment. Jean Bergonie was a French physician.

Cataphoresis or Ionic Medication
We cannot determine the precise nature of this treatment but Stedman's Medical Dictionary defines Cataphoresis as *'movement of positively charged particles in a solution towards a cathode'*. This is what we would call electrolysis.

D'Arsonval High Frequency Treatment
D'Arsonval of Paris was a respected specialist in hydrotherapy, working in the late 19th century. He conducted a number of experiments and designed equipment including a portable calorimeter for assessing fever in a patient. His high frequency treatment involved the use of electrical current and was a form of Diathermy.

Diathermy
Application of high frequency electric currents to produce heat in the deep tissues of the body. Also described in terms of High Frequency Currents (10 & 20 Mins) and Static Currents (10 & 20 Mins). Used for the relief of pain, to improve circulation and increase the range of joint movement.

Dowsing Radiant Light & Heat Treatment
This was prescribed for the treatment of stiff and painful joints and a range of additional complaints including rheumatism, gout, sciatica and lumbago. It consisted of a metal bed with heated panels and rows of light bulbs surrounding the patient.

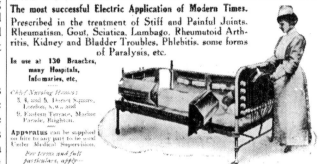

The DOWSING RADIANT HEAT TREATMENT
The most successful Electric Application of Modern Times.
Prescribed in the treatment of Stiff and Painful Joints. Rheumatism, Gout, Sciatica, Lumbago, Rheumatoid Arthritis, Kidney and Bladder Troubles, Phlebitis, some forms of Paralysis, etc.

In use at 130 Branches, many Hospitals, Infirmaries, etc.

Apparatus can be supplied to hire to any part to be used Under Medical Supervision.

For terms and full particulars, apply.

THE DOWSING RADIANT HEAT CO. LTD., 91 & 93 Baker St., London, W.1

Installed at the Thermal Baths, Buxton.

Electric Light Bath
A wardrobe-like piece of apparatus which was lined with rows of electric light bulbs on its inner surfaces. The patient stood in the middle of this arrangement and in certain cases a spray douche was applied. Various other forms of apparatus, using rows of light bulbs, were devised to treat parts of the body, for example, the spine, trunk, legs and feet.

Electro 4 Cell Schnee bath
We assume, given the name, that this treatment used the application of direct current from a battery to the bath in the same way as the electro-water bath.

Electro-Water Bath
With the patient immersed in a metal bath at a temperature of 92-98° F (33-36°C), electricity was applied to the body via a stationary head plate and sliding metallic electrodes on each side. The strength of the current, which could be either direct or alternating, was increased to such a level that a distinct tingling sensation could be detected by the patient. Recommended for the treatment of insomnia. It is not difficult to imagine that this treatment had the potential to be a permanent solution to the problem of insomnia!

Galvanising
Application of direct electrical current to the body, sometimes in association with shampooing (Massaging)

Appendix 2

Official analysis of Buxton's mineral water

	mg/l
Calcium	55
Magnesium	19
Sodium	24
Potassium	1
Bicarbonates	248
Chloride	42
Sulphates	23
Nitrates	0.1
Iron	0
Aluminium	0

Total dissolved solids at 180°C   280   PH at source   7.4

By kind permission of Buxton Mineral Water Company Limited

Appendix 3

Temperature Conversion

In the text we have used the Fahrenheit (F) measurement which was most frequently used in this country until decimalisation. We have given a Celsius (C) conversion in brackets. The conversion formulæ used are:

$$C = (F - 32) \times 0.55$$

$$F = \frac{9 \times C}{5} + 32$$

Square & George Hotel, Buxton.